Book 2

MAXIMIZE YOUR POTENTIAL
THROUGH THE POWER OF
YOUR SUBCONSCIOUS MIND
TO CREATE

Wealth and Success

Other Hay House Classics Titles by Dr. Joseph Murphy

Believe in Yourself
Miracles of Your Mind
Techniques in Prayer Therapy

Other Books in the MAXIMIZE YOUR POTENTIAL Series:

Book 1: *Maximize Your Potential Through the
Power of Your Subconscious Mind to Overcome Fear and Worry*

Book 3: *Maximize Your Potential Through the Power of Your
Subconscious Mind to Develop Self-Confidence and Self-Esteem*

Book 4: *Maximize Your Potential Through the
Power of Your Subconscious Mind for Health and Vitality*

Book 5: *Maximize Your Potential Through the
Power of Your Subconscious Mind for a More Spiritual Life*

Book 6: *Maximize Your Potential Through the
Power of Your Subconscious Mind for an Enriched Life*

⊨✢⊨

All of the above are available at your local bookstore,
or may be ordered by visiting:

Hay House USA: **www.hayhouse.com®**
Hay House Australia: **www.hayhouse.com.au**
Hay House UK: **www.hayhouse.co.uk**
Hay House South Africa: **www.hayhouse.co.za**
Hay House India: **www.hayhouse.co.in**

Book 2

MAXIMIZE YOUR POTENTIAL
THROUGH THE POWER OF
YOUR SUBCONSCIOUS MIND
TO CREATE

Wealth and Success

One of a Series of Six Books
by
Dr. Joseph Murphy

Edited and Updated for the 21st Century
by Arthur R. Pell, Ph.D.

HAY HOUSE, INC.
Carlsbad, California • New York City
London • Sydney • Johannesburg
Vancouver • Hong Kong • New Delhi

DR. JOSEPH MURPHY

Maximize Your Potential Through the Power of Your Subconscious Mind to Create Wealth and Success is one of a series of six books by Joseph Murphy, D.D., Ph.D., edited and updated for the 21st century by Arthur R. Pell, Ph.D. Copyright © 2005 The James A. Boyer Revocable Trust. Exclusive worldwide rights in all languages available only through JMW Group Inc.

Published and distributed in the United States by: Hay House, Inc.: www.hay house.com • **Published and distributed in Australia by:** Hay House Australia Pty. Ltd.: www.hayhouse.com.au • **Published and distributed in the United Kingdom by:** Hay House UK, Ltd.: www.hayhouse.co.uk • **Published and distributed in the Republic of South Africa by:** Hay House SA (Pty), Ltd.: www.hayhouse.co.za • **Distributed in Canada by:** Raincoast: www.raincoast.com • **Published in India by:** Hay House Publishers India: www.hayhouse.co.in

Library of Congress Cataloging-in-Publication Data

Murphy, Joseph, 1898–1981
  Maximize your potential through the power of your subconscious mind to create wealth and success / by Joseph Murphy ; edited and updated for the 21st century by Arthur R. Pell.
    p. cm. -- (Maximize your potential series ; bk. 2)
  ISBN-13: 978-1-4019-1215-4 (tradepaper) 1. New Thought. 2. Success--Psychological aspects. I. Pell, Arthur R. II. Title.
  BF639.M8316 2007
  154.2--dc22

                                                      2006019659

ISBN: 978-1-4019-1215-4

10 09 08 07   4 3 2 1
1st Hay House edition, November 2007

Printed in the United States of America

CONTENTS

———

Introduction to the Series vii

Preface xix

Chapter 1:   The Master Key to Wealth 1

Chapter 2:   Realize Your Desire 25

Chapter 3:   Programming Your Subconscious 33

Chapter 4:   The Wonderful Power of Decision 47

Chapter 5:   The Wonders of a Disciplined Imagination 65

Chapter 6:   There's No Free Lunch 77

Chapter 7:   "Why Did This Happen to Me?" 93

Chapter 8:   Praise: A Way to Prosperity 101

Chapter 9:   Why Your Beliefs Make You Rich or Poor 105

Chapter 10:   The Golden Rule 113

Chapter 11:   Your Future: The Art of Looking Forward 121

Biography of Joseph Murphy 127

Introduction to the Series

*W*ake up and live! No one is destined to be unhappy or consumed with fear and worry, live in poverty, suffer ill health, and feel rejected and inferior. God created all humans in His image and has given us the power to overcome adversity and attain happiness, harmony, health, and prosperity.

You have within you the power to enrich your life! How to do this is no secret. It has been preached, written about, and practiced for millennia. You will find it in the works of the ancient philosophers, and all of the great religions have preached it. It is in the Hebrew scriptures, the Christian Gospels, Greek philosophy, the Muslim Koran, the Buddhist sutras, the Hindu Bhagavad Gita, and the writings of Confucius and Lao-tzu. You will find it in the works of modern psychologists and theologians.

This is the basis of the philosophy of Dr. Joseph Murphy, one of the great inspirational writers and lecturers of the 20th century. He was not just a clergyman, but also a major figure in the modern interpretation of scriptures and other religious writings. As minister-director of the Church of Divine Science in Los Angeles, his lectures and sermons were attended by 1,300 to 1,500 people every Sunday, and millions tuned in to his daily radio program. He wrote more than 30 books, and his most well-known one, *The Power of Your Subconscious Mind,* was first published in 1963 and became an immediate bestseller. It was acclaimed as one of the greatest self-help guides ever written. Millions of copies have, and continue to be, sold all over the world.

Following the success of this book, Dr. Murphy lectured to audiences of thousands in several countries. In his lectures he pointed out how real people have radically improved their lives by applying specific aspects of his concepts, and he provided practical guidelines on how all people can enrich themselves.

Dr. Murphy was a proponent of the New Thought movement, which was developed in the late 19th and early 20th century by many philosophers and deep thinkers who studied it and preached, wrote, and practiced a new way of looking at life. By combining metaphysical, spiritual, and pragmatic approaches to the way we think and live, they uncovered the secret for attaining what we truly desire.

This philosophy wasn't a religion in the traditional sense, but it was based on an unconditional belief in a higher being, an eternal presence: God. It was called by various names, such as "New Thought" and "New Civilization."

The proponents of New Thought or New Civilization preached a fresh idea of life that makes use of methods that lead to perfected results. They based their thinking on the concept that the human soul is connected with the atomic mind of universal substance, which links our lives with the universal law of supply, and we have the power to use it to enrich our lives. To achieve our goals, we must work, and through this working, we may suffer the thorns and heartaches of humankind. We can do all these things only as we have found the law and worked out an understanding of the principles that God seemed to have written in riddles in the past.

The New Thought concept can be summed up in these words:

You can become what you want to be.

All that we achieve and all that we fail to achieve is the direct result of our own thoughts. In a just and ordered universe, where loss of balance would mean total destruction, individual responsibility must be absolute. Our weaknesses, strengths, purity, and impurity are ours alone. They are brought about by ourselves and not by another. They can only be altered by ourselves, and never by anyone else. All of our happiness and suffering evolve from within. As we think, so we are; as we continue to think, so we remain. The only way we can rise, conquer, and achieve is by lifting up our thoughts. The only reason we may remain weak, abject, and miserable is to *refuse* to elevate our minds.

All achievements—whether in the business, intellectual, or spiritual world—are the result of definitely directed thought; and are governed by the same law and are reached by the same method. The only difference lies in the object of attainment. Those who would accomplish little must sacrifice little; those who would achieve much must sacrifice much; those who would attain a great deal must sacrifice a great deal.

New Thought means a new life: a way of living that is healthier, happier, and more fulfilling in every possible manner and expression.

Actually, there is nothing new in this, for it is as old and time-honored as humankind. It is novel to us when we discover the truths of life that set us free from lack, limitation, and unhappiness. At that moment, New Thought becomes a recurring, expanding awareness of the creative power within; of mind-principle; and of our Divine potential to be, to do, and to express more of our individual and natural abilities, aptitudes, and talents. The central mind-principle is that new thoughts, ideas, attitudes, and beliefs create new conditions. According to our beliefs, is it done unto us—good, bad, or indifferent. The essence of New Thought consists of the continual renewing of our mind, that we may manifest what is good, acceptable, and the perfect will of God.

To prove is to know surely, and to have trustworthy knowledge and experience. The truths of New Thought are practical, easy to demonstrate, and within the realm of accomplishment of everyone—if and when he or she chooses. All that is required is an open mind and a willing heart: open to hearing old truths presented in a different way; willing to change and to relinquish outmoded beliefs and to accept unfamiliar ideas and concepts—to have a higher vision of life, or a healing presence within.

The rebirth of our mind constitutes the entire purpose and practice of New Thought. Without this ongoing daily renewal, there can be no change. New Thought establishes and realizes an entirely new attitude and consciousness that inspires and enables us to enter into "life more abundant."

We have within us limitless powers to choose and to decide, and complete freedom to be conformed or to be transformed. To be conformed is to live according to that which already has taken or been given form—that which is visible and apparent to our own senses, including the ideas, opinions, beliefs, and edicts of others. It is to live and to be governed "by the fleeting and unstable fashions and conditions of the moment." The very word *conformed* suggests that our present environment has shape, and that we do not and should not deny its existence. All around us there are injustices, improprieties, and inequalities. We may and do find ourselves involved in them at times, and we should face them with courage and honesty and do our best to resolve them with the integrity and intelligence that we now possess.

Generally, the world accepts and believes that our environment is the cause of our present condition and circumstance—and the usual reaction and tendency is to drift into a state of acquiescence and quiet acceptance of the present. This is conformity of the worst kind: the consciousness of defeatism. It's worse because it is self-imposed. It is giving all power and attention to the outer, manifested state. New Thought insists on the renewal of the mind, and the recognition and acknowledgment of our responsibility in life—our ability to respond to the truths we now know.

One of the most active and effective of New Thought teachers, Charles Fillmore, co-founder of the Unity School of Christianity, was a firm believer in personal responsibility. In his book *The Revealing Word,* he wrote (simply, and without equivocation): "Our consciousness is our real environment. The outer environment is always in correspondence to our consciousness."

Anyone who is open and willing to accept the responsibility has begun the transformation—the renewal of the mind that enables us to participate in our transformed life. "To transform" is "to change from one condition or state to another" (which is qualitatively better and more fulfilling) "from lack to abundance; loneliness to companionship; limitation to fullness; illness to vibrant health"—through this indwelling wisdom and power, the healing presence will remain within.

True and granted, there are some things we cannot change: the movement of the planets, the turn of the seasons, the pull of the oceans and tides, and the apparent rising and setting of the sun. Neither can we alter the minds and thoughts of another person—but we can change ourselves.

Who can prevent or inhibit the movement of your imagination and will? Only you can give that power to another. You can be transformed by the renewing of your mind. This is the key to a new life. You're a recording machine; and all the beliefs, impressions, opinions, and ideas accepted by you are impressed in your deeper subconscious. But you can change. You can begin now to fill your mind with noble and Godlike patterns of thoughts, and align yourself with the Infinite Spirit within. Claim beauty, love, peace, wisdom, creative ideas . . . and the Infinite will respond accordingly, transforming your mind, body, and circumstances. Your thought is the medium between your spirit, your body, and the material world.

The transformation begins as we meditate, think upon, and absorb into our mentality those qualities that we desire to experience and express. Theoretical knowledge is good and necessary. We should understand what we're doing and why. However, actual change depends entirely on stirring up the gifts within—the invisible and intangible spiritual power given fully to every one of us.

This, and only this, ultimately breaks up and dissolves the very real claims and bondage of past unhappiness and distress. In addition, it heals the wounds of heartbreak and emotional pain. We all desire and require peace of mind—the greatest gift—in order to bring it into our environment. Mentally and emotionally, contemplate Divine peace, filling our mind and heart, our entire being. First say, "Peace be unto this house."

To contemplate lack of peace, disharmony, unhappiness, and discord, and expect peace to manifest is to expect the apple seed to grow into a pear. It makes little or no sense, and it violates all sense of reason, but it is the way of the world. We must seek ways to change our minds—to repent where necessary. As a result, renewal will occur, following naturally. It is desirable and necessary to transform our lives by ceasing to conform to the world's way of choosing or deciding, according to the events already formed and manifested.

The word *metaphysical* has become a synonym for the modern, organized movement. It was first used by Aristotle. Considered by some to have been his greatest writing, his 13th volume was simply entitled *Metaphysics*. The dictionary definition is: "Beyond natural science; the science of pure being." *Meta-* means "above, or beyond." *Metaphysics,* then, means "above or beyond physics"— "above or beyond the physical," the world of form. "Meta" is above that; it is the spirit of the mind, which is behind all things.

Biblically, the spirit of God is good. "They that worship God worship the spirit, or truth." When we have the spirit of goodness, truth, beauty, love, and goodwill, it is actually the Divine in us, moving through us. God, truth, life, energy, spirit—can it not be defined? How can it be? "To define it is to limit it."

This is expressed in a beautiful old meditation:

> *Ever the same in my innermost being: eternal, absolutely one, whole, complete, perfect; I AM indivisible, timeless, shapeless, ageless—without face, form, or figure. I AM the silent brooding presence, fixed in the hearts of all men (and women).*

We must believe and accept that whatever we imagine and feel to be true will come to pass; whatever we desire for another, we are wishing for ourselves.

Emerson wrote: "We become what we think about all day long." In other words and most simply stated: Spirit, thought, mind, and meta is the expression of creative presence and power—and as in nature (physical laws), any force can be used two ways. For example, water can clean us or drown us; electricity can make life easier or more deadly. The Bible says: "I form the light, and create darkness; I make peace, and evil; I, the Lord, do all these things—I wound, I heal; I bless, I curse."

No angry deity is punishing us; we punish ourselves by misuse of the mind. We also are blessed (benefited) when we comprehend this fundamental principle and presence, and learn and accept a new thought or an entire concept.

Metaphysics, then, is the study of causation—concerned not with the effect that is now manifest, but rather with that which is causing the result. This discipline approaches spiritual ideas as scientists approach the world of form, just as they investigate the mind or causation from which the visible is formed, or derived. If a mind is changed, or a cause is changed, the effect is changed.

The strength and beauty of metaphysics, in my opinion, is that it is not confined to any one particular creed, but is universal. One can be a Jew, Christian, Muslim, or Buddhist and yet still be a metaphysician.

There are poets, scientists, and philosophers who claim no creed; their belief is metaphysical.

Jesus was a master metaphysician—he understood the mind and employed it to lift up, inspire, and heal others.

When Mahatma Gandhi (the "great-souled" one) was asked what his religion was, he replied, "I am a Christian . . . a Jew . . . a Buddhist . . . a Hindu . . . I AM all these things."

The term *New Thought* has become a popular, generalized term. Composed of a very large number of churches, centers, prayer groups, and institutions, this has become a metaphysical movement that reveals the oneness or unity of humankind with Infinite life . . . with the innate dignity, worth, or value of every individual. In fact, and in truth, the emphasis is on the individual rather than on an organizational body or function. But as mentioned, there is nothing new in New Thought. Metaphysics is actually the oldest of all religious approaches. It reveals our purpose to express God, and the greater measures of the Good: "I AM come to bring you life and that more abundantly." It reveals our identity: "children of the infinite" who are loved and have spiritual value as necessary parts of the Creative Holy (whole) One.

Metaphysics enables and assists us to return to our Divine Source, and ends the sense of separation and feeling of alienation; of wandering in a barren, unfriendly desert wasteland. This approach has always been, is now, and ever will be available to all—patiently waiting our discovery and revelation.

Many thousands have been introduced to New Thought through one or another of its advocates. Its formation was gradual, and usually considered to have begun with Phineas P. Quimby. In a fascinating article in *New Thought* magazine, Quimby wrote about his work in 1837. After experimenting with mesmerism for a period of years, he concluded that it was not the hypnotism itself, but the conditioning of the subconscious, which led to the resulting changes. Although Quimby had very little formal education, he had a brilliant, investigative mind and was an original thinker. In addition, he was a prolific writer and diarist. Records have been published detailing the development of his findings. He eventually became a wonderful student of the Bible and duplicated two-thirds of the Old and New Testament healings. He found that there was much confusion about the true meaning of many biblical passages, which caused misunderstanding and misinterpretation of Jesus Christ.

All through the 20th century, so many inspired teachers, authors, ministers, and lecturers contributed to the New Thought movement. Dr. Charles E. Braden, of the University of Chicago, called these people "spirits in rebellion" because these men and women were truly breaking free from existing dogmatism, rituals, and creeds. (Rebelling at inconsistencies in the old traditions led some individuals to fear religion.) Dr. Braden became discontent with the status quo and refused to conform any longer.

New Thought is an individual practice of the truths of life—a gradual, continuing process. We can learn a bit today, and even more tomorrow. Never will we experience a point where there is nothing more to be discovered. It is infinite, boundless, and eternal. We have all the time we need—eternity. Many of us are impatient with ourselves, and with what we consider our failures. Looking back, though, we discover that these have been periods of learning, and we needn't make these mistakes again. Progress may seem ever so slow: "In patience, possess ye your soul."

In Dr. Murphy's book *Pray Your Way Through It: The Revelation,* he commented that heaven was noted as being "awareness," and Earth, "manifestation." Your new heaven is your revised point of view—your new dimension of consciousness. When we see—that is, see *spiritually,* we then realize that in the absolute, all is blessed, harmony, boundless love, wisdom, complete peace, and perfection. Identify with these truths, calm the sea of fear; have confidence and faith, and become stronger and surer.

In the books in this series, Dr. Murphy has synthesized the profundities of this power and has put them into an easily understood and pragmatic form so that you can apply them immediately to your life. As Dr. Murphy was a Protestant minister, many of his examples and citations come from the Bible. The concepts these passages illustrate should not be viewed as sectarian. Indeed, their messages are universal and are preached in most religions and philosophies. He often reiterated that the essence of knowledge is in the law of life and belief. It is not Catholic, Protestant, Muslim, or Hindu; it is pure and simple faith: "Do unto others accordingly."

Dr. Murphy's wife, Dr. Jean Murphy, continued his ministry after his death in 1981. In a lecture she gave in 1986, quoting her late husband, she reiterated his philosophy:

> I want to teach men and women of their Divine Origin, and the powers pregnant within them. I want to inform them that this power is within and that they are their own saviors and capable of achieving their own salvation. This is the message of the Bible, and nine-tenths of our confusion today is due to wrongful, literal interpretation of the life-transforming truths offered in it.
>
> I want to reach the majority, the man on the street, the woman overburdened with duty and suppression of her talents and abilities. I want to help others at every stage or level of consciousness to learn of the wonders within.

She said of her husband: "He was a practical mystic, possessed by the intellect of a scholar, the mind of a successful executive, the heart of the poet." His message summed up was: "You are the king, the ruler of your world, for you are one with God."

Joseph Murphy was a firm believer that it was God's plan for people to be healthy, prosperous, and happy. He countered those theologians and others who claimed that desire is evil and urged people to crush it. He said that extinction of our longings means apathy—no feeling, no action. He preached that desire is a gift of God. It is healthy and wholesome to want to become more and better than we were yesterday . . . in the areas of health, abundance, companionship, security, and more. How could these be wrong?

Desire is behind all progress. Without it, nothing would be accomplished. It is the creative power and must be channeled constructively. For example, if one is poor, yearning for wealth wells up from within; if one is ill, there is a wish for health; if lonely, there is a desire for companionship and love.

We must believe that we can improve our lives. A belief— whether it is true, false, or merely indifferent—sustained over a period of time becomes assimilated and is incorporated into our mentality. Unless countermanded by faith of an opposite nature, sooner or later it takes form and is expressed or experienced as fact, form, condition, circumstance, and the events of life. We have the power within us to change negative beliefs to positive ones, and thereby change ourselves for the better.

You give the command and your subconscious mind will faithfully obey it. You will get a reaction or response according to the nature of the thought you hold in your conscious mind. Psychologists and psychiatrists point out that when thoughts are conveyed to your subconscious mind, impressions are made in your brain cells. As soon as this part of you accepts any idea, it proceeds to put it into effect immediately. It works by association of ideas and uses every bit of knowledge that you have gathered in your lifetime to bring about its purpose. It draws on the infinite power, energy, and wisdom within you, lining up all the laws of nature to get its way. Sometimes it seems to bring about an immediate solution to your difficulties, but at other times it may take days, weeks, or longer.

The habitual thinking of your conscious mind establishes deep grooves in your subconscious mind. This is very favorable for you if your recurring thoughts are harmonious, peaceful, and constructive. On the other hand, if you have indulged in fear, worry, and other destructive concepts, the remedy is to recognize the omnipotence of your subconscious and decree freedom, happiness, perfect health, and prosperity. Your subconscious mind, being creative and one with your Divine Source, will proceed to create the freedom and happiness that you have earnestly declared.

Now for the first time, Dr. Murphy's lectures have been combined, edited, and updated in six new books that bring his teachings into the 21st century. To enhance and augment this original text, we have incorporated material from some of Jean Murphy's lectures and have added examples of people whose success reflects Dr. Murphy's philosophy.

The other works in this series are listed on the second page of this book, but just reading them will not improve your state of being. To truly maximize your potential, you must study these principles, take them to heart, integrate them into your mentality, and apply them as an integral part of your approach to every aspect of your life.

— **Arthur R. Pell, Ph.D.,** editor

─╬─ ─╬─

Editor's Note: While updating these works, at times I have added current examples (that is, events and situations that may have occurred after Joseph Murphy's death) showing how basic principles presented by the author are still valid.

Preface

*H*ave you ever imagined what it would be like if you were wealthy and could live a life of luxury? Wealth seems so remote to most people, yet there are countless examples throughout history of men and women who by their own efforts rose from the depths of poverty to great riches.

Are you destined to be poor? To paraphrase Shakespeare, some people are born wealthy, some achieve wealth, and some have wealth thrust upon them. There are some who are fortunate to have wealthy parents who gave them all that money could buy—but many of these people lost their parents' wealth through their own bad judgment. There are others who have had wealth thrust upon them by winning a lottery or some other windfall. However, most of us are not so lucky. In order to become wealthy, we have to achieve through our own intelligence, diligence, creativity, and commitment. None of us is destined to be poor. Wealth is all around us, and all we need do to achieve it is to seek and follow the road that will lead us there.

There is nothing wrong with wanting to get rich. The desire for riches is really the desire for a richer, fuller, and more abundant life; and that desire is praiseworthy. People who don't want to live more abundantly are abnormal, and people who don't desire to have enough money to buy all they want are abnormal.

Why be satisfied with just enough to make ends meet when you can enjoy the riches of the infinite? In this book you will learn to make friends with money, and you will always have a surplus. Your desire to be rich is a desire for a fuller, happier, and more wonderful life. It's a cosmic urge that is good—indeed, very good. Begin to see money in its true significance. It's a symbol of exchange. It represents freedom from want; and can provide beauty, luxury, abundance, and refinement.

One of the reasons why many people don't have more money is that they're silently or openly condemning it. They refer to money as "filthy lucre," or they believe that "the love of money is the root of all evil" or similar fallacies. Another reason they don't prosper is that they have a sneaky, subconscious feeling that there's some virtue in poverty. This feeling may stem from early childhood training, superstition, and a false interpretation of the scriptures.

There's no virtue in poverty. It's a disease like any other mental disease. If you were physically ill, you would accept that there was something wrong with you and would seek help or do something about it at once. Likewise, if you don't have money constantly circulating in your life, there's something radically wrong with you. You must take action—at once.

God doesn't want you to live in a hovel or to go hungry. God wants you to be happy, prosperous, and successful. God is always successful in His undertakings, whether He makes a star or a cosmos.

Let go of all superstitious beliefs about money immediately. Don't ever regard money as evil or filthy. If you do, you cause it to take wings and fly away from you. Remember that you lose what you condemn.

It's perfectly right that you should desire to be rich; if you are a normal man or woman, you cannot help doing so. It's perfectly right that you should program the power of your subconscious mind to improve your financial condition. It's your duty to yourself, God, and humanity, for you can render to God and humanity no greater service than to make the most of yourself.

There are now, and there always will be, some people who accept poverty as their natural lot. However, they aren't doomed to that state, because the tools are there to help them lift themselves from poverty by increasing development and understanding.

Those who know life understand this first cause of poverty.

When we look more deeply, we see that until the last person with this scarcity consciousness has died, the poverty-stricken will continue to be in our midst, because deep in their minds and souls they still look upon themselves as beggars.

The second cause of poverty is the false education of the past, which, instead of hastening the evolution of humankind, has served to keep it in bondage. Many religions contain as part of their dogma the teaching that poverty is an inevitable condition for most people. They preach, "The poor will always be with us." Some sects even claim that for many, poverty is predestined and should be accepted as a way of life.

Some interpreters of spirituality preach that to be poor is to be spiritual—that it's "easier for the camel to go through the eye of a needle than for a rich person to enter the kingdom of Heaven." Believing this lie, they live in misery, hoping and trusting that in some far-off future, a heaven will be given to them for their pain. According to some religions, such as those of the East, persons born in poverty will always live in poverty—hoping that by being obedient and humble, they will be reborn in their next life in a higher caste with greater wealth.

These old obsessions held the multitude in their iron clasp for centuries. Strange as it may seem, even now in this enlightened century, there are still many people hugging to their hearts this old delusion and dragging on in penury and despair, resisting the compelling force of higher revelation. There are thousands of poor people today who still cling to this old tradition, only from false religious ardor and a lack of self-investigation.

In this book, Dr. Joseph Murphy reexamines these concepts and makes clear to his readers that poverty isn't the natural state of humankind and certainly isn't the will of God. He will show you how, through positive thinking, meditation, prayer, and faith in your God-given self, you will achieve success in your endeavors, prosperity, and wealth.

— **Arthur R. Pell, Ph.D.,** editor

Chapter One

The Master Key to Wealth

*T*he whole world and all its treasures—the sea, air, and earth—were here when you were born. Begin to think of the untold and undiscovered riches all around you, waiting for the Intelligence that exists to bring them forth. Look at wealth as the air you breathe. Get that attitude of mind. Emerson expressed this succinctly when asked by a woman how she could prosper. He took her down to the ocean and told her to take a look. She observed that the ocean contains a countless number of drops of water and an extraordinary variety of sea life. Emerson suggested that if she also looked at wealth as an infinite supply, she would always enjoy an abundance of it.

Realize that wealth is like a tide forever flowing out and forever flowing back. Wealth is an idea in your mind and a mental attitude. For example, a sales manager told me that an associate of his sold a million-dollar idea for expansion to an organization. You can have an idea worth a fortune, too. The sales manager also told me that there are more millionaires in the United States now than at any time in the history of the country.

You can have an idea worth a fortune; yes, you can. Moreover, you're here to release the splendor within you and surround yourself with luxury, beauty, and the riches of life. Learn that it's necessary to have the right attitude toward money, wealth, food, and clothing. When you really make friends with wealth, you will always have a surplus of it. It's normal and natural for you to desire a fuller, richer, happier, and more wonderful life. Look upon money as God's idea, maintaining the economic health of the nations of the world.

When money is circulating freely in your life, you are economically healthy—in the same way that when your blood is circulating freely, your body is healthy. Begin now to see money in its true significance and its role in life as a symbol of exchange. That's all it is. It has taken many forms down through the ages. Money to you should mean freedom from want. It should mean beauty, luxury, abundance, security, and refinement. You are entitled to it.

Are some people destined or chosen to enjoy the riches of this world while others are fated to suffer hardship and deprivation? In truth, absolutely not. Money is a clear result of the Creative Power and Presence within us, which moment by moment responds to us, producing the conditions and circumstances of our daily lives—creating according to the deeper thoughts of our subconscious minds and the meditations of our hearts.

Those who enjoy the true abundance and prosperity of life are those who are aware of the creative power of mind and thought. They continually impress their subconscious minds with ideas of spiritual, mental, and material abundance—prosperity and plenty—and that deeper mind automatically causes abundance to manifest in their experience. True abundance is "honest gain."

This is the great and universal law of life—operative and effective in everyone. This has always been true, and will be forever. Our deep-seated, heartfelt beliefs and opinions become our experience. If we're convinced that we live in a generous, intelligent, and infinitely productive universe—governed by a loving God—our conviction will be reflected in our circumstances and activities.

Likewise, if our dominant conviction is that we aren't worthy of infinite wealth, that we're doomed or fated to remain without, and that wealth is for others, this conviction will be reflected in our circumstances and activities.

Beliefs are the primary determinants of whether we're rich in material abundance or poor. Beliefs are the reason why "the rich get richer and the poor get poorer." Thoughts of abundance produce abundance; thoughts of lack produce lack. I know that focusing on abundance and wealth when one is suffering from a condition of insufficiency requires a tremendous effort. It requires a sustained and continuous belief that prosperity will come. However, the person who practices this disciplined thinking will inevitably achieve wealth.

The key phrase is *disciplined thinking.* Discipline of the mind begins when we're eager, willing, and yearning for Truth. We must "renew" our mind—think in a new way. This requires that we examine and understand our heartfelt beliefs and opinions as well as our ideals and aspirations. These dreams are within the realm of possibility.

Being poor is an attitude. For example, a young woman, a very good writer who had several articles accepted for publication, said to me one time, "I don't write for money."

I replied, "What's wrong with money? It's true that your sole motivation for writing may not be money, but your writing is worthy of monetary compensation. What you write inspires, lifts up, and encourages others. When you adopt the right attitude, money will automatically come to you freely and copiously."

However, this young woman actually disliked money and had a subconscious belief that there's some virtue in poverty. Once she referred to money as *filthy lucre*—a belief going back, I suppose, to her early years, when she probably heard her mother or somebody else say that money is evil, or that the love of money is the root of all evil. On the contrary, it's a rank superstition to say that money is evil or is filthy lucre and that poverty is noble. I explained to her that there's no evil in the universe and that good and evil are in the thoughts and motivations of people. All "evil" comes from misinterpretations of life and misuse of the laws of mind. In other words, the only evil is ignorance. It would be foolish to say that platinum, silver, gold, or a dollar bill is evil. How absurd, grotesque, and stupid that is! A piece of paper such as a hundred-dollar bill is innocuous.

The woman realized that her condemnation of money caused it to fly *from* her instead of *to* her, and she decided that she would change her view of money and allow more of it into her life. Here's the simple affirmation she used to increase her wealth: "My writings go forth to bless, heal, inspire, elevate, and dignify the minds and hearts of men and women. I am Divinely compensated in a wonderful way. I look upon money as Divine substance, for everything is made from the One Spirit. I know that matter and Spirit are one. Money is constantly circulating in my life, and I use it wisely and constructively. Money flows to me freely, joyously, and endlessly. Money is an idea in the mind of God. It is very good."

That's a wonderful prayer. It eradicates that superstitious nonsense about money being evil, poverty being virtuous, and the Lord loving the poor. All of these beliefs are frightful ignorance—and that's all they are. This young lady's changed attitude toward money has worked wonders in her life. Her income tripled in three months, which was just the beginning of her financial prosperity. A positive attitude toward money will work wonders in your life, too.

The crucial step in creating this positive attitude is to give your allegiance, loyalty, and trust not to created things, but to the Creator, the Eternal Source of everything in the universe. This is the Source of your own breath, your life, the hair on your head, and your heartbeat—and the Source of the sun, the moon, the stars, and the earth that you walk on. In biblical language, to *love* means to give your allegiance to this Source of all things, which is God, the Living Spirit or Life Principle in you.

Unfortunately, even the most well-intentioned people misunderstand the law of abundance. For instance, some years ago I talked with a minister who had a very good following. He had an excellent knowledge of the laws of mind and was able to impart this knowledge to others. But he could never make ends meet. He rationalized his plight by quoting from the New Testament: "For the love of money is a root of all kinds of evil," forgetting that later in the same chapter, it says that God gives riches to people so that they can help others. In other words, the minister took the statement about money being a root of evil out of context. In fact, the Bible enjoins people to place their trust or faith in the Living God "who richly provides us with everything for our enjoyment."

I pointed out to this minister how he was completely misinterpreting the scripture in pronouncing pieces of paper or metal evil, when in fact these are neutral substances, for there is nothing good or bad but thinking makes it so. He began to see all the good he could do with more money for his wife, family, and parishioners. He changed his attitude and let go of his superstition. He began to claim boldly, regularly, and systematically: "Infinite Spirit reveals better ways for me to serve. I am inspired and illumined from On High, and I give a Divine transfusion, a faith and confidence in the One Presence and Power, to all those who hear me. I look upon money as God's idea, and it's constantly circulating in my life and the lives of all the people who surround me. We use it wisely, judiciously, and constructively under God's guidance and wisdom."

This young clergyman made a habit of repeating this prayer, knowing that it would activate the powers of his subconscious mind. Today he has a beautiful church, a radio program, and all the money he needs for his personal and professional life. I can assure you that he no longer criticizes money.

There's nothing wrong with money, not a thing in the world, but it's not the sole aim in life. To make money the only purpose in your life would constitute an error or a wrong choice. There wouldn't be anything evil in it, but you'd be imbalanced and lopsided. You're here to lead a balanced life. You must also claim peace, harmony, beauty, guidance, love, joy, and wholeness in all phases of your life. How can you live without courage, faith, love, goodwill, and joy in this world today?

You must also express your hidden talents and find your true place in life. You must experience the joy of contributing to the growth, happiness, and success of others—for we are all here to give. Give your talents to the world. God gave you everything. God gave you Himself. You have a tremendous debt to pay, because you owe everything you have to the Infinite; therefore, you are here to give life and love and truth. You are here to row the boat, put your hands on the wheel, and contribute to the success and happiness of not only your children, but also of the whole world.

As you apply the laws of your subconscious in the right way, you can have all the money you want and still have peace of mind, harmony, and serenity. You can do a lot of good with your money. You can use it wisely and constructively, like anything in nature.

Follow this technique that I'm going to outline for you and you will never want for wealth all the days of your life, for it's the master key to wealth. The first step is to get clear in your mind that God or the Life Principle is the Source of the universe, the galaxies in space, and everything you see, including the stars in the sky, the mountains, the lakes, the deposits in the earth, the oceans, and all the animals and plants. The Life Principle gave birth to you; and all the powers, qualities, and attributes of God are within you, including energy, vitality, health, and creativity. It's as easy for God to manifest wealth in your life as it is for this One Source to reveal itself as a blade of grass or a flake of snow. Come to a simple conclusion that everything you see and are aware of came out of the Invisible Mind of the Infinite, and that everything that has ever been invented or created came out of this Invisible Mind. Also know that the human mind and the mind of God are one, for there is only one mind. This mind is common to all people. Everyone is an inlet and outlet to all that is.

The second step: Decide now to engrave in your subconscious mind the idea of wealth. Ideas are conveyed to the subconscious by repetition, faith, and expectancy. By repeating a thought pattern or an idea over and over again, it becomes automatic, and your subconscious will be compelled to express wealth. You must believe in what you're affirming. It's not mumbo jumbo or an idle affirmation. You must believe in the power of your words—just as you believe that when you put flower seeds in the ground, flowers will grow—not corn or zucchini or radishes. The seeds are the thoughts that you deposit in your subconscious mind, and you will get exactly what you plant.

Realize that what you're affirming is like the apple seed you deposit in the ground. You can imagine the seed going from your conscious to your subconscious mind and being reproduced on the screen of space. By watering and fertilizing these seeds, you accelerate their growth. Know what you're doing and why you're doing it. Know that there's an infinite abundance in the Universe. Walk down the street and you can see it. Can you count the flowers along the road as you drive? Can you count the grains of sand on the seashore? Can you count the stars in the sky?

The third step is to repeat the following affirmation for about five minutes in the morning and evening: "I am now writing in my subconscious mind the idea of God's wealth. God is the Source of my supply, and I know that God is the Life Principle within me, and I know that I am alive. All my needs are met at every moment of time and point in space. God's wealth flows freely, joyously, and ceaselessly into my experience, and I give thanks for God's riches forever circulating in my experience."

Step four: When thoughts of lack come to you, such as, "I can't afford that trip" or "I can't pay that bill," reverse these negative statements immediately in your mind by affirming, "God is my instant and everlasting supply, and that bill is paid in Divine order." If a negative thought comes to you 50 times in one hour, reverse it each time by thinking and affirming, "God is my instant supply meeting that need right now." After a while, the thought of financial lack will lose all momentum and you will find that your subconscious is being conditioned for wealth. If you look at a new car, for example, never say, "I can't buy that" or "I can't afford it." Your subconscious takes you literally and blocks all your good. On the contrary, say to yourself, "That car is for sale. It's a Divine idea, and I accept it in Divine order through Divine love." This is the master key to wealth. It's impossible for any sincere person to practice this technique and not have all the wealth needed all the days of their lives.

Using the above technique, you set the law of opulence in operation. It will work for you as well as for anybody else, because the law of mind is no respecter of persons. Your thoughts make you wealthy or poor. Choose the riches of life right here and right now.

I know a sales representative who used this law of mind to achieve great success. This man was a brilliant college graduate. He knew his products very well. He was in a lucrative territory but was making only $10,000 annually in commissions. His sales manager felt that he should be able to double or triple his sales and referred him to me for counseling. In talking with the young man, I found that he was down on himself. He had developed a subconscious belief that he was only worth $10,000 a year. He said that he had been born in a poverty-stricken home and that his parents had told him he was destined to be poor. His stepfather had always told him, "You'll never amount to anything. You're dumb, you're stupid." These thoughts were accepted by his impressionable mind, and he was experiencing his subconscious belief in lack and limitation.

I explained to him that he could change his subconscious mind by feeding it with life-giving patterns. I gave him a simple affirmation to use and told him that he should under no circumstances deny what he affirmed, because his subconscious mind would accept what he really believed. He affirmed every morning before going to work: "I am born to succeed. I am born to win. The Infinite within me cannot fail. Divine law and order govern my life. Divine peace fills my soul and Divine love saturates my mind. Infinite Intelligence guides me in all ways. God's riches flow to me freely, joyously, endlessly, and ceaselessly. I am moving forward and growing mentally, spiritually, financially, and in all other ways. I know these truths are sinking into my subconscious mind, and I know and believe that they will manifest in abundance."

A few years later when I met this young man again, I discovered that he had been transformed. He had absorbed the ideas that we had discussed. He said, "I'm appreciating life now and wonderful things have happened. I have an income of $75,000 this year, five times greater than the previous year." He has learned the simple truth that whatever he inscribes on his subconscious mind becomes effective and functional in his life. This power of the subconscious mind is also within you. Your subconscious mind accepts your convictions, so believe in God's wealth and riches, which are all around you.

I recently met a man who used the power of the subconscious mind to increase his income fivefold. He was earning $40,000 a year working in a bank, which was quite satisfactory, but he wanted to make more money for his wife and children. He made a practice of affirming: "God is my instant supply. I am Divinely guided in all ways. Infinite Spirit opens up a new door." He told me that an opportunity came to him some months ago and that he now is working in sales on a commission basis. He had enough faith in himself to leave the secure bank job and move on. He's now earning $200,000 a year. He's able to do great things, and he and his family are enjoying a wonderful life.

Wealth was an idea in his mind, and everything you look at is an idea. A radio is an idea. A television is an idea. An automobile is an idea. Anything that you might desire is an idea that you can bring to fruition in your life.

Use the following meditation for assurance and achieving financial wealth:

I know that my faith in God determines my future. My faith in God means my faith in all things good. I unite myself now with true ideas, and I know the future will be the image and likeness of my habitual thinking. As I think in my heart or subconscious, so I will be. From this moment forward, my thoughts are on whatever is true, just, lovely, and good. Day and night I meditate on these things, and I know these seeds, which are thoughts that I habitually dwell upon, will become a rich harvest for me. I am the captain of my soul; I am the master of my fate.

You see, prayers and affirmations are not for the purpose of changing or influencing God or the Living Spirit. God is the same yesterday, today, and forever. You don't change God, but you align yourself mentally with that which was always true. You don't create harmony; harmony is. You don't create love; God is love, and the love of God is within you. You don't create peace; God is peace, and God indwells you. But you must claim that the peace of God floods your mind. You must claim that the harmony of God is in your home. Harmony is in your pocketbook, your business, and all phases of your life. Everything good is available to each of us. Our prayers and affirmations are for the purpose of bringing our own mind to the point where we can accept the gifts that were given to us from the foundation of time, for God is the giver and the gift.

A person's use of God's guiding principle determines whether he or she will achieve prosperity. For example, if you send two geologists to Utah to seek out precious metals, one may look for years and find nothing, while the other finds a vein of uranium or silver in the same territory in the first five minutes. Where was the wealth? The wealth was in the mind of the second person, who believed in the guiding principle. The other person found nothing even though it was right there.

This guiding principle will also lead *you* to the precious things you seek. You don't need to work on conditions; you only need to work on yourself. The only place you can cure lack and limitation is in your own mind. Your world is an exact reflection of your inner state of mind. Whatever you ask for when you pray, believe that you have received it, and you shall have it. This belief is the basis of all successful prayer, whether for the healing of our bodies, or for prosperity, success, and achievement. Once you convince your deeper mind that you have the thing you want, it will proceed immediately to bring it to pass.

You might ask me, "How can I convince my deeper mind, my subconscious, that I have riches or any other good thing when my common sense tells me that bills are piling up, creditors are after me, the bank is calling up about my unpaid mortgage, and so on?" If you keep thinking about debts and obligations and how much you owe, you will only magnify your misery. But here's a truth about the laws of your mind: Your deeper mind accepts as fact whatever you repeat to it often enough in convincing tones.

When you learned how to walk, you had no doubt that no matter how many times you fell, you would eventually learn to walk without stumbling. Your subconscious accepted your belief and you did learn to walk. The same principle works in praying for wealth and anything else. Once your subconscious accepts a statement about your growing wealth as fact, it proceeds to do everything possible to bring riches to you. That's the whole purpose of affirmation—to convince yourself of the truth of that which you affirm. Then your deeper mind will bring these things to pass.

A woman who came to my office misunderstood the application of the law of attraction. She told me, "Oh, I got an affirmation from someone, saying 'I'm rich and prosperous now. I'm successful and very wealthy.' That affirmation just made me much more aware of my need." Unfortunately, she had believed more in poverty and lack than she had in the riches all around her.

I explained: "You must turn away from that pattern; change your belief. Your subconscious accepts what you believe. Look around you. Realize that God created you and the whole world. It's an invisible spirit within you. It created your heartbeat, the air you breathe, the water you drink, and the food you eat. Therefore, turn away from thoughts of limitation and turn within and say, 'I recognize the Eternal Source of my supply. God is the Source of my supply. All my needs—spiritual, mental, and material—are met at every moment of time and point in space. God's wealth is circulating in my life and there is always a surplus. By day and by night I'm advancing and growing spiritually in every way.'"

She began to realize the Source of the infinite ocean of supply, of the very hair on her head, the grass, the hay in the field, the cattle, and a thousand hills. She aligned herself with this Source and realized that she was writing in her subconscious mind the idea of wealth, growth, and prosperity. She changed her belief in poverty, which was a false belief, to a belief in the endless riches all around her.

Don't you know that enough fruit rots in the tropics to feed all humanity? Nature is lavish, extravagant, and bountiful. God richly gave you all things to enjoy. Heretofore you asked for nothing; now ask that your joy might be full. In the Bible, you see, to ask is to claim. You claim it boldly, but you know what you're doing and why you're doing it.

If you have a lot of debts and obligations and a lot of bills to pay, don't worry about them. Turn to the Source, which is endless. Remember the farmer who said: "I don't worry about the weeds. The grain is growing, and it will kill all the weeds." That's what the farmer tells you. Likewise, as you focus on your good and the Eternal Source of your supply—whether it's mental, spiritual, or financial—turn to it and give thanks for endless supply, then all the weeds will be killed. Thoughts of lack and limitation will die in you, and God will multiply your good exceedingly.

Bring joy into your life. Pray for joy by claiming it. "The joy of the Lord is your strength," the Bible says. Repeat this to yourself and after a while you'll be amazed by what will happen to your bloodstream and to your general circulation. Don't keep analyzing problems or gritting your teeth about them. Just know that joy is the spirit and expression of life. Don't work like a horse to achieve joy. No willpower or muscle power is used in this mental and spiritual therapeutic technique. Just know and claim that the joy of the Lord is flowing through you now, and wonders will happen as you pray. Freedom and peace of mind will be yours. If you have peace of mind, you will have peace in your pocketbook, your home, and your relationship with people, for peace is the power at the heart of God.

A woman told me about her experience with affirmative prayer. She said to me, "I was blocked financially. I had reached the point where I didn't have enough money for food for the children. All I had was $5. I held it in my hand and said, 'God will multiply this exceedingly according to his riches and glory, and I'm now filled with the riches of the Infinite. All my needs are instantaneously met now and all the days of my life.'"

The woman said that she repeated her affirmation for about half an hour and that a great sense of peace came over her.

"I spent the five dollars freely for food," she said, "and the owner of the market asked me if I wanted to work there as a cashier since their previous cashier had just quit. I accepted the job and shortly afterward I married the owner, my boss, and we are experiencing all the riches of life."

This woman looked to the Source and believed her affirmation. It wasn't just idle words. She didn't know *how* her prayer would be answered, because one can never know the workings of the subconscious, but she believed in her heart in the blessings of the Infinite. Her good was magnified and multiplied exceedingly because the subconscious always magnifies what you give attention to.

You don't gain the ear of God through vain repetitions. You must know what you're doing and why you're doing it. You must know that your conscious mind is a pen and that you're writing or engraving something in your subconscious mind. Whatever you impress your subconscious mind with will be expressed on the screen of space. It will come forth as form, experience, and events—good or bad. So make sure you plant that which is lovely and good.

There's a Presence and a Power within you, and you can use it. You can stir up the gift of God within you, for God is the giver and the gift, and everything has been given to you. Therefore, you can tune in and claim guidance, right action, beauty, love, peace, abundance, and security. You can say to yourself, "God's ideas unfold within me, bringing me harmony, health, peace, and joy." If you are in business or are an artist or inventor, just sit down quietly and say, "God reveals new creative, wonderful ideas to me that bless humanity in countless ways." Then watch the wonderful ideas come to you. And they will come, because when you call, Source answers. Remember what it says in the Bible: "Call upon me and I will answer you. I will be with you in trouble. I will set you On High because you have known my name."

The nature of Infinite Intelligence is responsiveness. Call and the response comes. Constantly affirm, feel, and believe that God multiplies your good, and you will be enriched every moment of the day—spiritually, mentally, intellectually, financially, and socially. For there's no end to the glory of daily living. Watch the wonders that will happen as you impress these truths in your subconscious mind. As you read these words, let these truths sink into your subconscious. You're engraving them. The more often you do this, the faster you will impregnate your deeper mind, and you will experience a glorious future.

Watch your thoughts. Never talk about economic lack and limitation. Never talk about being poor or in want. It's very foolish to talk to your neighbors or relatives about hard times, financial problems, and similar matters. Count your blessings and begin to think prosperous thoughts. Talk about the Divine riches present everywhere and realize that the feeling of wealth produces wealth. When you talk about not having enough to go around and how you must cut corners and eat the cheapest meat, you're only impoverishing yourself. Use the money freely. Release it with joy and realize that God's wealth flows to you in avalanches of abundance.

Look to the Source. As you turn to the Divine Presence within you, the response will come. It's written: *God cares for you.* You will find neighbors, strangers, and associates adding to your good and also to your supply of material things. Make it a practice to pray for Divine guidance in all your ways, and believe that God, or the Supreme Intelligence, is supplying all your needs according to His riches in glory. Claim it boldly. Come to the throne of grace.

Grace, when its mystique is removed, is simply the orderly reflection of your habitual thinking and imagery. In other words, it's the Supreme Intelligence that responds to your conscious thinking and imagery. Pray for Divine guidance, therefore, in all your ways. As you make a habit of this attitude of mind, you'll find that the invisible law of opulence can and will produce visible riches for you.

Recently a doctor told me that her constant prayer is as follows: "I live in the joyous expectancy of the best, and invariably the best comes to me." She said that her favorite Bible verse is: 'He giveth to all life and breath, and all things." She has learned that she isn't dependent on people for joy, health, success, happiness, or peace of mind. She looks to the Living Spirit Almighty within her for promotion, achievement, wealth, success, and happiness. You can also contemplate promotion, success, and achievement; and the spirit of the Almighty will move in your behalf, compelling you to express fully what you meditate on. Let go now and permit the Infinite One to open up new doors for you and allow riches and wonders in your life.

In praying, avoid struggle and strain. Don't try to force things. Can you make a seed grow? You can't. Plant it in the ground and it will grow. The oak is in the acorn and the apple is in the apple seed. The archetype of pattern is in the seed, but you must deposit it in the soil where it undergoes transformation and bequeaths its energy to another form of itself. When a spiritual-minded man looks at an acorn, he sees a forest.

Your conscious mind is prone to look at external conditions and tends to continually struggle and resist. If you are worried, fearful, and anxious, you inhibit your good and bring about blocks, delays, and impediments in your life. Remember, however, that it's the quiet mind that gets things done. Quiet your body periodically; tell it to be still and relaxed. It has to obey you. Your body has no self-conscious intelligence, no volition, and no will. It moves when moved upon. You can play a melody of God on your body. When your conscious mind is quiet and receptive, the wisdom of your subconscious rises to the surface mind and you receive your solution.

A beautician told me that the secret of her success is daily quieting her mind and praying. Every morning prior to opening her beauty salon, she has a quiet period in which she affirms: "God's peace fills my soul. God's love saturates my whole being. God guides, prospers, and inspires me. I am illumined from On High. His healing love flows from me to all my clients. Divine love comes in my door. Divine love goes out of my door. All those who come into my salon are blessed, healed, and inspired. The Infinite Healing Presence saturates the whole place. This is the day the Lord has made, and I rejoice and give thanks for the countless blessings that come to my clients and myself."

She has this prayer written out on a card and reiterates these truths every morning. At night she gives thanks for all her clients, claiming that they are guided, prosperous, happy, and harmonious and that God in His love flows through each one, filling up all the empty vessels in their lives. She stated to me that after praying in this way for three months, she had far more clients than she could handle. She had to hire three additional beauty operators. She had discovered the riches of effective prayer and is prospering beyond her fondest dreams.

I knew another couple who used affirmative prayer to save their marriage. The husband, a sales manager, told me that he had been fired because of excessive drinking on the job and because he was involved with one of the secretaries in the office. He was very distressed, dejected, and worried about his wife, his income, and his future.

In talking with his wife later, I discovered that she was a chronic nagger and had tried unsuccessfully to dominate and control her husband. She was abnormally jealous and very possessive. She clocked him in every evening, creating a scene if he wasn't home at a certain hour. The husband was emotionally and spiritually immature and didn't handle the matter at all constructively. He deeply resented her nagging and retaliated by drinking and becoming involved with another woman. He said to me, "I just wanted to get even with her."

Both of them agreed that it takes two to make a go of marriage, and it takes two to prosper. If a husband and wife will agree on prosperity and success, they will prosper. They will have all the money they need to do what they want to do when they want to do it. And when you have all the wealth you need to do what you want to do when you want to do it, you are as rich as a Rockefeller. Both of them agreed to start a prayer process, realizing that as they prayed for each other, there couldn't possibly be any bitterness, hostility, or resentment, as Divine love casts out everything unlike itself.

She prayed in the morning and in the evening as follows: "My husband is God's man. God is guiding him to his true place. What he is seeking is seeking him. Divine love fills his soul. Divine peace fills his mind and heart. He is prospered in all ways—spiritually, mentally, financially, and socially. By day and by night he is advancing in all ways—for life itself is growth. There is harmony, peace, love, and understanding between us. It is Divine right action and Divine peace operating in our lives."

He prayed for his wife night and morning as follows: "My wife is God's child. She is a daughter of the Infinite, a child of Eternity. Divine love fills her soul, and it is written: God cares for her. Divine love, peace, harmony, and joy flow through her at all times. She is Divinely guided and prospered in all her ways. There is harmony, peace, love, and understanding between us. I salute the Divinity in her, and she salutes the Divinity in me."

As both of them became relaxed and peaceful about the situation, they realized that only good could come out of this situation. Soon he received a phone call from the president of the company, who had heard that the man had reconciled with his wife. At the same time, the president praised him for his past achievements and accomplishments. Actually, the sales manager's wife, without his knowledge, had visited the president of the company and had told him the whole story—how happy they now were and how the other woman had vanished from his life. She told him how they were now praying together. The president was impressed and decided to rehire his former employee. The couple discovered the riches of scientific prayer and found that their married life became happy and prosperous.

You can know if you've succeeded in prayer by the way you feel. If you remain worried or anxious or if you're wondering how, when, and through what source your answer will come, you're meddling and blocking your prayer. This indicates that you don't really trust the wisdom of your subconscious. Avoid nagging yourself all day long, or even from time to time. When you think of your desire, lightness of touch is important. Remind yourself that Infinite Intelligence is taking care of it in Divine order far better than you could using your conscious mind.

For example, if you say, "I need $5,000 by the 15th of next month" or "The judge must make a decision for me by the first of the month or I'll lose my home," you're creating fear, anxiety, and tension. What will that do? It will bring about blocks, delays, impediments, and difficulties in your life. Instead, always go to the Source. Remember that peace and confidence shall be your strength. Go to a place of absolute rest in your mind and say to yourself: "It is done unto me as I believe. All things be ready if the mind be so. According to my faith is it done unto me. The light of God shines in me. The peace of the Everlasting God fills my soul. In quiet and confidence shall be my strength. God gave me richly all things to enjoy. With God all things are possible."

Read a psalm, such as the 23rd or 91st, and go over it quietly, peacefully, and lovingly. You'll get to a point of rest and peace in your mind. You'll realize that God is never late and that God is your instant and everlasting supply, guiding and directing you, revealing everything you need to know, and opening up the door for you. You'll know that God's riches are circulating in your life and that there's always a surplus. When you go to the Source, the way will open up, the dawn will appear, and the shadows will flee. But you won't get an answer by worrying and being fearful. This will only attract more lack and greater difficulties. Dwell, therefore, upon the truths of God, such as: God is absolute peace, total harmony, boundless wisdom, and infinite intelligence. God is the ever-living one, the all-wise one, the all-knowing one, the self-renewing one, and the source of all blessings.

This practice will quiet your mind and give you peace. And when the mind is at peace, it gets the answer. For in quietness and in confidence shall be your strength. And God knows only the answer. So learn to let go and relax. Don't give power to the externals or conditions; instead, give power and allegiance to the Infinite, the Presence and Power within you.

When you're seeking wealth, prosperity, success, or a spiritual healing, feel that you're immersed in the Holy Omnipresence, like you're in the ocean or in a swimming pool, and realize that the

Golden River of life, love, truth, and beauty is flowing through you now, transforming your whole being into a pattern of harmony, love, peace, and abundance. Feel yourself swimming in the great ocean of life. That sense of oneness will restore you.

The following meditation will bring many wonderful things into your life. Say:

> *These truths are sinking into my subconscious mind. I picture them going from my conscious to my subconscious like seeds that I deposit in the soil. I know that I create my own destiny. My faith is in the Infinite Being, Which created all things, and my faith in God is my fortune. This means an abiding faith in all things good. I live in the joyous expectancy of the best, and only the best comes to me. I know the harvest I will reap in the future, because all my thoughts are God's thoughts. The power of God is with my thoughts of good. My thoughts are the seeds of goodness, truth, beauty, and abundance. I now place my thoughts of love, peace, joy, success, abundance, security, and goodwill in the garden of my mind. This is God's garden. The glory and beauty of God will be expressed in my life, and I know that my garden will yield an abundant harvest. From this moment forward, I express life, love, and truth. I am radiantly happy and prosperous in all my ways, and God multiplies my good exceedingly.*

Never be envious or jealous of another person's wealth, promotion, or jewels, for that would impoverish you. Jealousy would attract lack and limitation to you. Instead, rejoice in their success and their prosperity and wish for them greater riches—for what you wish for the other you're wishing for yourself. When you think positively about the other, you create abundance in your own mind, body, experience, and pocketbook. This is why you need to rejoice in the success and prosperity that millions of others have. In order to truly prosper, it's necessary that you become a channel through which the Life Principle flows freely, harmoniously, joyously, and lovingly.

One young man who consulted me had experienced a poverty complex for many years but had received no answers to his prayer. He had prayed for prosperity, but the fear of poverty continually weighed upon his mind. Naturally, he attracted more lack and limitation than prosperity.

After talking to me, he began to realize that every thought is creative unless it's neutralized by an opposing thought of greater intensity. Furthermore, he realized that his thoughts and beliefs about poverty were greater than his belief in the infinite riches all around him. Consequently, he changed his thoughts and kept them changed. I wrote out a prosperity prayer for him, as follows. It will benefit you:

> *I know that there is only One Source, the Life Principle or Living Spirit, from which all things flow. It created the universe and all things therein contained. I am a focal point of the Divine Presence. My mind is open and receptive. I am a free-flowing channel for harmony, beauty, guidance, wealth, and the riches of the Infinite. I know that wealth, health, and success are released from within and appear in the without. I am now in harmony with the infinite riches within and without, and I know these thoughts are sinking into my subconscious mind and will be reflected on the screen of space. I wish for everyone all the blessings of life. I am open and receptive to the Divine riches—spiritual, mental, and material—and they flow to me in avalanches of abundance.*

This young man focused his thoughts on God's riches rather than on poverty. He made it a special point to never deny what he affirmed. Many people pray for wealth and then deny it an hour later. They say, "I can't afford this. I can't make ends meet." They're making a mockery of their prayer. They're like the man who gets into a taxi in New York going to the airport, and on the way says to the taxi driver, "Oh, take me back home; I forgot my passport." So he goes back home and they set off for the airport again, and the man says, "Oh, I'd better go to my club; I forgot my wallet." So the taxi driver takes him to his club to get his wallet, and they set off again for the airport. Then the man says, "Oh, I forgot some letters at my grandmother's," and off he goes to the grandmother's. He gives half a dozen directions to the taxi driver in just half an hour. Finally, the taxi driver takes him to the police station, because he realizes that the man is mentally disturbed.

This is the way in which millions of people pray—even those in the New Thought movement. They give half a dozen directions to their subconscious mind in half an hour or half a day. The subconscious is so confused and perplexed that it doesn't know what to do, so it doesn't do anything. As a result, you feel frustration. Instead, stop contradicting what you've affirmed—you don't put a seed in the ground and then dig it up, and you shouldn't offer a prayer and then take it back.

The young man ultimately focused his thoughts on God's riches rather than poverty, and he stopped saying, "I can't afford . . ." or "I can't buy that piano or that car." Never use the word *can't*. Can't is the only devil in the universe. Your subconscious takes you literally and blocks all your good. In a month's time, his whole life was transformed. He offered affirmative prayers in the morning and evening for about ten minutes, slowly and quietly engraving them in his mind . . . knowing what he was doing, believing what he was doing, and understanding that he was actually writing these truths in his subconscious mind, causing it to release hidden treasures. Although this man had been a salesman for ten years with rather dim prospects for the future, suddenly he was made a sales manager at $50,000 a year plus benefits.

The subconscious has ways that you know not of. It's impossible to impregnate your subconscious with the idea of wealth and be poor. It's impossible to impregnate your subconscious with the idea of success and not succeed; the Infinite cannot fail. You were born to triumph. Let your prayer be: "By day and by night, I am advancing and growing. God gave me richly all things to enjoy."

In a Nutshell

When money is circulating freely in your life, you're financially healthy—in the same way that when your blood is circulating freely, you're physically healthy.

To accumulate money to the exclusion of everything else causes one to become imbalanced, lopsided, and frustrated. However, as you apply the laws of your subconscious in the right way, you can have all the money you want and still have peace of mind, harmony, and wholeness.

God is the Source of your supply of energy, vitality, health, and creative ideas. God is the Source of the sun, the air you breathe, the apple you eat, and the money in your pocket.

Say every day: "I am born to succeed. I am born to win. The Infinite within me cannot fail. Divine law and order govern my life. Divine peace fills my soul. Divine love saturates my mind. Infinite Intelligence guides me in all ways. God's riches flow to me freely, joyously, endlessly, and ceaselessly. I am advancing and growing—mentally, spiritually, financially, and in all other ways. I know that these truths are sinking into my subconscious mind, and I know and believe they will grow and manifest."

Constantly affirm, feel, and believe that God multiplies your good exceedingly and you will be enriched every moment of the day, for there's no end to the glory of daily living. Watch the wonders that will happen as you impress these truths in your subconscious mind.

Offer this prayer daily:

I know that there is only One Source, the Life Principle or the Living Spirit, from which all things flow. It created the Universe and all things therein contained. I am a focal point of the Divine Presence. My mind is open and receptive. I am a free-flowing channel for harmony, beauty, guidance, wealth, and the riches of the Infinite. I know that wealth, health, and success are released from within and appear in the without. I am now in harmony with the infinite riches within and without, and I know these thoughts are sinking into my subconscious mind and will be reflected on the screen of space. I wish for everyone all the blessings of life. I am open and receptive to Divine riches—spiritual, mental, and material—and they flow to me in avalanches of abundance.

※ ※ ※

Chapter Two

---•◦•---

Realize Your Desire

*D*esire is a gift of God and is the push of the Life Principle within you. Desire is the Creative power; it must be channeled and directed wisely. Desire and its fulfillment take place in your own mind. It's due to desire that we jump out of the way of an oncoming bus. We do this because we have a basic desire to preserve our life. Farmers plant seeds because of their desire to obtain food for themselves and their families. We build airplanes and spaceships out of our desire to explore the world. Desire is the nudge of the Infinite, propelling us toward something that will make our life fuller and happier.

Some people believe that it's wrong to have desires. Is it really acceptable to acknowledge our desire to live a better life than we now have? Is it all right to long for more, to progress and prosper when there is so much suffering in the world? These are perfectly legitimate questions that must be resolved once and for all if we are to enjoy lasting, positive change. The belief that desire should be suppressed or annihilated is disastrous in its consequences. If people succeeded in suppressing all desire, good and evil would be the same to them. They would become dead to all feeling and lose all motivation to take action. Your desire means that you choose one thing in preference to another. Where desire is extinguished, no such capacity to choose can exist.

Thomas Troward, a 19th-century author of many spiritual textbooks, spent a number of years in India. He pointed out that

Indian devotees who resolve to crush all desire, for good and evil alike, became attenuated human forms—hopeless wrecks of what were once living beings. Troward also noted that the extinction of desire leads to apathy.

The suppression of desire is only good if the realization of that desire would cost us our integrity or come at the expense of others. A simple example: The desire for material wealth is good when we strive to gain it honestly, to provide for our family and children; however, if the acquisition of this wealth becomes so important to us that we take time for nothing else, neglect our families, and take advantage of others, then this desire has become misdirected. It's not the desire itself that is to blame; it's the corruption of the very meaning of abundance.

Failure to realize our desires to be, do, and have over a long period of time results in frustration and unhappiness. You aren't here to be unhappy; you're here to choose happiness, peace, prosperity, and all the blessings of life. Your desire enables you to say, "This is good; therefore, I choose it." For example, if you're poor, you desire wealth; if you're sick, you desire health. If you were in prison, you would desire freedom. If you were dying of thirst in the desert, you would desire water. All of these desires are natural and good.

There are no evil desires. However, you may misdirect or misinterpret the desire that wells up within you. The person who desires wealth may, in ignorance, fulfill that desire by killing a banker or robbing a store. This is misdirection of the desire, and that person will land in jail, charged with murder. Our desire for food is legitimate and normal, but hurting someone in order to get a loaf of bread is an act of violence.

If you've been victimized by the puritanical, repressive belief that desire is wrong, it's time to let go of this limiting thought and leave the spiritual darkness (ignorance of a generous universe). When we accept that there's an Infinite Intelligence within us that created the Universe and that it can fulfill all our desires, we overcome a sense of opposition and frustration. Then we know that there's a Power within us that will lift us up and set us on the high road to happiness, health, peace of mind, and the realization of our fondest dreams—without depriving any other person of his blessings.

Our world is a wilderness or desert that might be made into a beautiful garden, a lush vineyard, or a nourishing field of wheat. Our mind is a rich and fertile field that can be cultivated to produce plants of beauty that will replace the brambles and weeds in our lives. According to our desires, we can create a wonderful life and world.

When the farmer plants seeds in the ground and waters and nurtures them lovingly, the power of the Source or God transforms them into a bountiful crop. In the same way, whatever you plant in your mind in the way of thought, feeling, and imagination grows to become your reality. When we seed our mind with thoughts of abundance, and nurture them with our prayers and belief in God, our reward is our harvest of increased prosperity. On the other hand, thoughts of lack and limitation will result in a crop of negative situations and scarcity.

The seed is God's miracle. Drop it in a furrow and it disappears. Provided with sufficient water, it gestates in the darkness of the soil and is transformed into a plant or tree. The blueprint for its manifestation is contained in the seed, just as our thoughts contain the blueprint for the way our lives take shape. An idea or thought in the conscious, reasoning mind that is entertained regularly—and not contradicted or counteracted by another thought or opposing idea—gestates in the deeper mind and comes forth as our experiences. The extent to which an idea manifests depends on how much attention and emotion our conscious mind invests in it.

If you are disappointed, plant new ideas and allow them time to take root. They will grow and flourish. Plant life-giving, uplifting thoughts deep in your receptive mind and know that the generous, guiding, protective Deity brings these ideas to fruition. Your harvest will be magnificent beyond the fondest dreams and imaginings of your heart. Meditate on love, health, abundance of all description, and talents you may not even know you have. Riches of the spirit and material abundance can be yours.

Begin to regularly give thanks for your prosperity and good, and you'll find a change taking place. New ideas, contacts, and opportunities will appear. This is a wonderfully constructive use of the imaginative faculty, and you will experience good fortune. With God all things are possible. Whatever the mind can conceive of exists in potential reality in the Infinite Mind. God has given us everything necessary for our lives on Earth—an abundance of all that's required to enjoy fulfilling, joyous accomplishment. This law of the subconscious mind appears in the writing of ancient philosophers, the scriptures, and the texts of many religions.

Although we can't see the law of mind and the workings of the Source, we know that the Infinite Mind always responds. We know that Intelligence responds to our convictions—our deep-seated ideas and concepts. As the seed (the idea or thought) is nurtured (meditated and prayed about), the harvest (the reward) will be reaped. Intelligence cannot be seen; we can only see its results. For example, joy, kindness, anger, and hostility are invisible; only their effects are visible.

I worked with a man who used the power of the mind to transform his life. When he came to one of my lectures on the power of the subconscious mind, he was broke, out of work, and frightfully frustrated.

He had never heard a lecture on the mind, but said, "This makes sense," and went home to apply the teachings. He made a list of three things he wanted: a fulfilling job, an automobile, and money. He wanted to test the law of the subconscious, to find out for himself if the ideas in my lecture could help him. He established a daily practice of affirmative prayer, sticking to it long enough to give it a fair chance. This man knew that you don't learn to swim after one or two attempts.

He prayed as follows: "I know Infinite Intelligence responds to me. It is now revealing my true talents to me. I am aware of my hidden talents. I am receiving a wonderful income. I know the idea of my true vocation and its manifestation are one in Divine Mind. I follow the lead that comes into my conscious, reasoning mind. It's impossible for me to miss it. It comes in a clear and distinct way, and I recognize it." Within two weeks of the day his experiment began, he signed a contract for a job in San Francisco. He gave thanks and rejoiced in the law of his own mind. Then he went on to the next objective: a new car. Although he didn't have the money to buy one, he said to me, "I know I have the idea of a car. It's real, and I'm going to remain faithful to it. It must manifest." He offered daily affirmative prayers and soon won a car in a raffle.

Now he knew the secret of the subconscious: If he identified himself mentally and emotionally with an idea, the subconscious would bring it to pass. He was very thankful. The next request was more wealth. Each morning and evening during his prayer period, he gave thanks for God's riches circulating in his life, claiming that his idea of wealth was fulfilled. He fell in love with a wealthy widow in San Francisco, and she financed his new business. This man established a definite method of working, claiming each of his desires as already fulfilled.

Another person I know who used the law of the mind with great success is a young lad who works at the radio station where I broadcast. He told me that he decreed that his subconscious mind would reveal to him the perfect plan for going to the annual convention of an organization he belongs to. He prayed about this, and soon the way opened up and he was invited to the convention with all expenses paid.

He also told me that last year he decreed that the Infinite Intelligence in his subconscious would reveal the perfect plan for a trip to Europe, allowing him to visit many countries. The desire was fulfilled when his relatives offered to pay all his traveling expenses. Although he didn't have a cent in his pocket, he used his deeper mind to bring about his desired results.

You also have the unqualified capacity to go to that limitless storehouse within you. Claim what you want, feel it, and rejoice in it—and it will come to pass. Cultivate trust and know that whatever you ask for in prayer, you shall receive. Decide now that you can do what you long to do and that you can be what you long to be. No enlightened person today believes that a cruel fate condemns us to poverty, sickness, misery, or suffering. That's a primitive belief and is stupid beyond words. It's silly to blame an Infinite Being for troubles when we bring them upon ourselves through our wrong thinking and our misuse of the law of mind. You can use the power of your subconscious negatively or constructively.

One of my colleagues, Dr. J. Kennedy Schultz, the president of Religious Science International, wrote about the importance of choosing positive thought:

> Ideas are great when they support life-giving, healing concepts as universally available, applicable and desirable. They are about such things as individual freedom, universal peace, unconditional love and ever-expanding productivity. Such ideas give renewed life to one and all. They are the substance that has let the human race come to live better and better over the eons of our existence. Such ideas have been re-introduced and professed anew in every generation by enough individuals to keep human life in this world moving forward, if ever so slowly, in spite of all the ignorance and cruelty that has plagued every age.

The God Presence is the Infinite Life Principle within you that always seeks to heal you. Its tendency is to restore you and illuminate your pathway. There's nothing keeping you in mediocrity, ill health, or a miserable condition but your own thoughts and false beliefs. Come out of the prison of fear, want, and loneliness. Cease thinking that God is an old man up in the sky with whiskers who is punishing you. That is gross ignorance, and ignorance is the only sin in this universe. God is the Infinite Presence, Power, and Intelligence that is always within you. This Divine Source can effortlessly restore your health as you offer affirmative prayers that your body is perfect, whole, and complete. Indeed, research today reveals that the hidden, underlying causes of physical maladies lie in the tangled depths of the mind—in frustrated rage, baffled desires, jealousies, and anxieties.

Your own thoughts and words color everything in your universe. Don't, therefore, criticize, condemn, or despise your body or the world. Your body is the temple of the Living God. Glorify God in your body and glorify God in the world, which is the dance and song of the Infinite Source. If you condemn anything in this world, you are demoting and depreciating yourself.

Realize that the spirit and body are one, and don't look down your nose at material things. Stop, once and for all, separating the Spirit of God from the flesh and blood of the world. They are one and the same. Einstein defined matter as "spirit, or energy, reduced to the point of visibility." The ancient Hindus 10,000 years ago also believed that spirit and matter are one. Matter is the lowest degree of Spirit, and Spirit is the highest degree of matter. An automobile is a spiritual idea in front of your door. A ham sandwich, when you are hungry, is an answer to your prayer and is also spiritual.

Let us have our meditation now:

At the center of my being is the peace of God. In this stillness I feel the strength, joy, and love of His Holy Presence. I realize that Infinite Intelligence leads and guides me in all my ways. It is a lamp unto my feet and a light upon my path. I ride the white horse, which is the Spirit of God moving in the waters of my mind. I take my attention away from any perceived problems and dwell upon the reality of the fulfilled desire. I see the accomplished fact and rejoice in it.

In a Nutshell

Desire is the push of the Infinite telling us something that, if we accept it, will make our life fuller and happier. Without desire and the expectation of benefit or gain, people don't take the actions that lead to advancements in the world.

Desire is a creative power that must be channeled and directed wisely. Desire and its fulfillment take place in your own mind. If you identify yourself mentally and emotionally with an idea, the subconscious will bring it to pass.

Come out of the prison of fear, want, and loneliness. Cease thinking that God is an old man up in the sky with whiskers, capriciously limiting your good. It's ignorant to say that God is punishing you and ignorance is the only sin in this universe. All punishment, misery, and suffering are the consequence of ignorance. It's silly to blame an Infinite Being for troubles when we bring them upon ourselves through our wrong thinking and our misuse of the law of mind.

God is the Infinite Presence, Power, and Intelligence within you. Realize that the Healing Presence is within you and that it can restore you. Realize that Intelligence leads and guides you in all your ways. Take your attention away from the problem and dwell upon the reality of the fulfilled desire.

ᴴ✝ᴴ ᴴ✝ᴴ ᴴ✝ᴴ

Chapter Three

Programming Your Subconscious

*I*n order to understand how you can create wealth through the power of your subconscious mind, let's carefully examine how the mind works. Imagine that a psychologist or psychiatrist hypnotizes you. In the state of hypnosis, your conscious, reasoning mind is suspended and your subconscious is amenable to suggestion. If the psychiatrist suggested to you that you were the President of the United States, your subconscious would accept the statement as true, because it doesn't reason, choose, or differentiate (as your conscious mind does). You would assume all the airs of importance and dignity that you associate with the Presidential position.

If you were allergic to timothy grass, and the psychiatrist placed a glass of distilled water under your nose while you were under hypnosis, telling you that it was timothy grass, you would generate all the symptoms of an allergic attack; your physical reactions would be the same as if the water were actually the grass that you're allergic to.

If you were then told that you were a beggar on skid row, your demeanor would immediately change and you would assume the attitude of humble suppliant, gripping an imaginary tin cup in your hand. In short, you may be made to believe anything about yourself because of the complete receptivity of the subconscious mind.

An important thing to remember is that your subconscious mind always accepts your conviction without question, whether your premise is true or absolutely false, as in the case of the pre-ceeding examples.

Unfortunately, from infancy on, the majority of us have been given many negative suggestions. *Negative programming* would be a better term. Not knowing how to reject or thwart these sugges-tions, we unconsciously accepted them. You might have been told: "Oh, you can't do that." Maybe someone said to you: "You'll never amount to anything," or "You shouldn't try that because you'll fail." Now you have an inferiority complex. Perhaps you have also heard: "It's not *what* you know but *who* you know," "The world is going to the dogs," "Never trust anyone," "When you get old, your memory fails," "Life is an endless grind," "Love is for the birds," "Nobody cares," "It's no use trying so hard," and "The world is getting worse all the time."

If you look back, you can easily recall how parents, friends, relatives, teachers, and others contributed to a campaign of nega-tive suggestions. Study the things that were said to you and you'll discover that the purpose of most of the messages was to control you or instill fear in you.

If you accept all these negative suggestions, you're program-ming your subconscious mind in a very harmful way. You then develop a sense of inferiority, inadequacy, and fear. Unless as an adult you program your subconscious mind constructively, the impressions made on you in the past can cause behavior patterns that lead to failure in your personal and professional life. Program-ming is a means of releasing yourself from the negative verbal conditioning that might otherwise make you unhappy.

For example, let's say that Charles is a sourpuss or has a nasty temper and wants to change this trait. One way that he can deal with this is to sit down every night and morning and affirm: "Every day I am becoming more and more lovable and understanding. I am now becoming a source of cheer, cordiality, and goodwill to all those around me, infecting them with good humor. This happy, joyous, and cheerful mood is now becoming my normal, natural state of mind, and I am grateful."

Charles can engrave these words in his subconscious and reprogram and redirect his mind. Since the subconscious is completely receptive, he will be compelled to become congenial and cordial—a man of goodwill. Whatever is impressed on the subconscious mind comes forth as form, experience, and conditions.

Pick up the newspaper and you can read dozens of items that could sow the seeds of futility, worry, anxiety, and impending doom. These fearful thoughts could cause you to lose your will to live. Know that you can reject all these negative suggestions by giving your subconscious mind constructive suggestions. Every morning you can sit quietly, get relaxed, and affirm: "Divine law and order govern my life. Divine right action reigns supreme. Divine success is mine. Divine harmony is mine. Divine peace fills my soul. Divine love saturates my whole being. Divine abundance is mine. Divine love goes before me today and every day, making straight, joyous, and glorious my way."

This is the way a marine captain programmed his subconscious mind during World War II. He reiterated these truths frequently. Every morning and every night, he repeated his own version of the 23rd Psalm:

> *The Lord is my pilot. I shall not drift. He lighteth me across the dark waters. He steereth me in the deep channels. He keepeth my log. He guideth me by the star of holiness for His namesake. Yea, though I sail amid the thunders and tempests of life, I shall dread no danger for thou art with me. Thy love and thy care, they shelter me. Thou preparest a harbor for me in the homeland of Eternity. Thou anointest the waves with oil. My ship rideth calmly. Surely, sunlight and starlight shall favor me on the voyage I take, and I will rest in the port of my God forever.*

Gradually, through repetition, faith, and expectancy, these thoughts entered his subconscious mind. Since whatever is expressed to the subconscious must express in life, he was therefore compelled to lead a life of harmony, peace, and love.

You can program your subconscious mind, too. Every morning before you step into your automobile, remind yourself that the Divine Source is the one driving and that you arrive safely at your destination. Program your mind to know that you are guided by the All-Knowing Infinite. As you announce these truths and believe in them, they sink into your subconscious mind and result in your having a safe and effortless journey—for the nature of your subconscious mind is to manifest your thoughts.

At a talk I gave at a Unity church in New Orleans, a woman told me a story that illustrates the power of the subconscious mind. She said that there was a man who used to come to her church and say quite frequently, "There are a lot of holdups in my neighborhood. My shop stays open rather late at night, and I'm going to be held up one of these nights. I'll probably be shot, too."

The church members told him, "Stop making these negative suggestions. Stop thinking along these lines."

Well, the shop owner didn't pay any attention and continued to dwell on danger. He kept programming his subconscious negatively, and he was eventually held up. He was also shot. He had programmed his subconscious the wrong way. He could have used the 91st Psalm and prayed,

I dwell in the secret place of the Most High. I abide in the shadow of the Almighty. I will say of the Lord: He is my refuge and my fortress. My God, in Him will I trust. Surely, He shall cover me with His feathers, and under His wing shall I rest. And the truth shall be my shield and buckler. I shall not be afraid for the terror by night or the arrow that flieth by day.

He could have reiterated these truths and realized that the love of God surrounded and enfolded him. He could have said to himself: "Thou art my hiding place. Thou wilt compass me about with songs of deliverance." Then he would have built up immunity to all harm, because prayers are spiritual antibodies.

Another woman who programmed her mind the wrong way was found raped and strangled in her apartment a few years ago.

The detective who investigated the case told me that in her apartment he found newspaper clippings about rape going back for 20 years. She had programmed her subconscious mind negatively and, as a result, experienced that which she feared.

Fear is faith upside down. Fear is faith in the wrong thing. For instance, one politician said to newspaper reporters: "I live in constant fear of assassination." He didn't know the laws of mind. He didn't know, perhaps, that he could cast out fear. *I will fear no evil, for Thou art with me. Thy rod and thy staff, they comfort me. One with God is a majority. If God be for me, who can be against me? Thou art my hiding place. Thou shalt compass me about with songs of deliverance.*

The politician could instead say, "I dwell in the secret place. The sacred circle of God's eternal love surrounds me. The whole armor of God surrounds me. Wherever I go, the light of God enfolds and enwraps me." He would render himself invulnerable, invincible, and impervious to all harm. That's the right way to program your subconscious mind. *As a man thinketh in his heart* [or subconscious] *so is he.*

Whatever is impressed in the subconscious is expressed in your life. Remember that when you're dealing with your subconscious, you're dealing with the power of the Almighty. It's the Power that moves the world and the galaxies in space. There's nothing to oppose it. If you think "poor" thoughts, you will always be poor. If you think "prosperous" thoughts, you will prosper. You're the one who's choosing. You mold and fashion your own destiny. Your faith should therefore be in the goodness and guidance of God, and in the beauty and glory of the Infinite.

I worked with a man who overcame his belief in lack and limitation. He told me that he wanted to succeed and advance in life, but in reality, he didn't. He had a subconscious pattern of failure. He had a sense of guilt and felt that he should be punished. With his conscious mind, yes, he worked very hard. But in his deeper mind he was programmed and conditioned for defeat. He had a sense of unworthiness and a belief that compelled him to fail.

Once this man realized that he was punishing himself, he began to change his beliefs. He started praying every morning and night: "I was born to win. I was born to succeed in my prayer life, my relationship with people, my chosen work, and in all phases of my life. The Infinite is within me, and the Infinite cannot fail. It is the power and wisdom of the Almighty moving through me. Success is mine. Harmony is mine. Wealth is mine. Beauty is mine. Divine love is mine. Abundance is mine."

He repeated these truths daily and reflected upon them. He reminded himself of them as he drove along the road and before he went in to see a customer. He announced these truths regularly and systematically, and he didn't deny what he affirmed. Gradually, he became a tremendous success, because he succeeded in impregnating his subconscious mind with the wonderful truth about himself.

If you plant life-affirming thoughts in your mind as regularly and systematically as this man did, wonders will also happen in your life, for the Infinite Power is within all of us. This All-Mighty Source knows no failure, and there's nothing to oppose, challenge, or thwart it.

As the Bible says: *I will put my laws into their mind, and write them in their hearts: and I will be to them a God, and they shall be to me a people.* All the powers of God are within you, and the laws and the truths of God are written in your own subjective mind. This Intelligence governs all the vital organs of your body, your breathing, the circulation of your blood, your digestion, and your heartbeat—all without any conscious effort on your part. When you were born, no one had to tell you how to find your mother's breast. There was a subjective wisdom guiding and directing you.

The great eternal truths were inscribed in our hearts before we were born, but many of us have been programmed with negative thoughts since birth. Millions of people have been programmed with certain fears, false beliefs, taboos, strictures, and superstitions. As Phineas Parkhurst Quimby, a pioneer in the New Thought movement, said, "Every child is like a little, white tablet. Everybody comes along and scribbles something on it, including grandmother, grandfather, clergyman, mother, father, sisters and brothers."

Many people have been taught that they are sinners in the hands of an angry God. I have talked to women who are beautiful and well educated but who have been programmed to think that it's a sin to use rouge or makeup of any kind or to wear gold. They also have been taught to believe that dancing, playing cards, and movies are the works of the devil. These women are frustrated, bottled up, inhibited, and unhappy. I tell them to wake up. I say, "There's nothing evil in dancing, playing cards, or anything of that nature. Nothing is good or bad, but thinking makes it so. Go ahead and learn to dance, for the Universe is the dance of God. Take lessons in golf, play music, and do all the things that you've been fearful of. Attend college, take lectures in public speaking, and meet men. Go out and take courses in Spanish and many other things. Learn a trade or profession and earn money. You're here to lead a full and happy life. You're here to have fun, joy, and creativity and to express yourself. You're also here to meditate and pray, of course."

Then I explain to them that they are frustrated, sick, and unhappy because their natural, good desires are being blocked. I say, "You've been brainwashed. You've been programmed negatively and destructively. The will of God for you is a greater measure of joy, happiness, love, and peace of mind." Every woman wants to be loved and cosseted and appreciated. She likes to receive attention. She wants to feel needed and wanted. And if she says she doesn't, she's sick.

These women have learned about the power of the subconscious and the law of attraction. You should see some of them now, going to the theater beautifully dressed. They wear lovely rings— sometimes wedding rings. They have transformed themselves and have reprogrammed their minds to accept greater joy and love.

I was taught when I was young that if a child were indoctrinated with a certain religious belief until about the age of seven, no one could change that belief. Of course, a belief *can* be changed, but it's rather difficult, because when we're young, we're impressionable and teachable. We don't usually have the sense to reject negative suggestions. We accept many false beliefs and erroneous concepts regarding God, life, and the universe. For instance, some people believe that every November they're going to get the flu. They attribute it to the climate, the change of seasons, and so on. Of course, because they have programmed their minds to get this illness and expect it every year, according to their belief it is done unto them. Someone with this negative belief in "flu season" will regularly get sick in November. Yet other members of his family, living in the same house and eating the same food, don't get the flu at all. Similarly, some people believe that the night air will give them a cold, or that if someone sneezes in the office they'll get the sniffles—and according to their belief it is done unto them. Others in the office exposed to the same germs don't get a cold.

It's all belief or negative conditioning. When a person sneezes in the office, it doesn't mean that you're going to catch a cold or that some germ is going to attack you. However, if you have created a belief in your mind that sneezing spreads germs, you will catch a cold. It's therefore wise to stop making laws for yourself that hurt you.

The power of suggestion can produce positive as well as negative results. Dr. David Seabury told me about a man who had lost the use of his legs and who had little formal education. Seabury decided to test the power of suggestion and told this man, "You are destined to become a great evangelist. God intended you to go forth and preach in a wonderful, wonderful way." This man became active in his particular church, and he did become an outstanding preacher. He accepted the belief that God had ordained him to become a great preacher. And according to his belief it was done to him. It was as simple as that.

How are you programming your subconscious mind? If you believe in a God of love and give this Living Spirit all your allegiance, devotion, and thoughts, you'll lead a charmed life. If you focus on negativity and calamity, you'll face a difficult life of deprivation. The alcoholic, for example, has repeatedly fed to himself thoughts about weakness, inadequacy, inferiority, and rejection. As he continues to make these negative suggestions to himself and continues to drink to bolster his courage, he's denying the Divinity and the power of the Almighty within him. After a while, through repeated negative suggestions, he has lost his sense of choice and become a compulsive drinker. Before, he could say, "Well, I'll have one or two drinks and that's all." Now he has lost that power. He has rejected the One Presence and Power and has implanted these negative suggestions by repetition into his deeper mind. He can change his thinking, but it will take some effort.

Let's look at Sally, who has become an alcoholic and lost her job because of it. It's not easy for her to overcome this addiction. She must truly want to give up drinking, of course, and make a clear-cut decision to do it. When her desire to stop drinking is greater than her desire to continue, she will be 75 percent healed. Then the power of the Almighty will back her up and move on her behalf. When she makes the decision to stop abusing alcohol, she claims that sobriety and peace of mind are hers. She says, "I decree this, I mean it, and I am absolutely sincere. It's irrevocable." Then she pictures herself doing what she loves to do. If she's an attorney, for example, she visualizes herself back in court pleading a case for a client, or behind the polished mahogany desk researching a case. She's perfectly groomed and well dressed. She's talking to the judge and going about her work.

When the desire comes to her to have a drink, she flashes the movie in her mind of living a successful life without alcohol, and the power of the Almighty backs her up. As she continues to think about freedom, peace of mind, and sobriety, she begins to feel joy and wonder. Her thoughts take root in her subconscious and come to pass. This is reprogramming her subconscious mind for health and sobriety. The power of the Almighty will take away the craving for alcohol and she will be free. Sally also needs to forgive herself for harboring negative thoughts in the past.

We're all here to grow, learn, and release the imprisoned splendor that's within. Joy is in mastery. We aren't born with our faculties fully developed, but are here to sharpen our mental and spiritual tools. We have the freedom to learn, choose, and overcome.

That's the way we discover our Divinity. There's no other way under the sun. You aren't compelled to be good. You aren't an animal governed by instinct only. Therefore, you have the opportunity to *choose* to become holy.

I hold before you an open door that no person can shut. Think about whatever is true, lovely, noble, and godlike. Think about these things all day long, and you can begin to recondition your mind. Picture yourself doing what you long to do, and your vision will begin to come true. As you continue to focus your attention on that which is wonderful and good, your deeper mind will respond and you will be compelled to move forward in the light, for the Almighty Power will move on your behalf.

As you drive along the road or go about your other routine tasks, repeat to yourself:

> *There is only One Power, One Presence, One Cause. It is boundless love, infinite intelligence, and absolute harmony. It is moving in me, through me, and all around me. I will fear no evil for thou art with me. Thy rod and thy staff, they comfort me. The Lord is my light and my salvation; whom shall I fear? The Lord is the strength of my life; of whom shall I be afraid?*

Keep on reiterating these truths morning, noon, and night, and they will sink into your subconscious. Out of the subconscious will come forth whatever you have impressed upon it, so see to it that nothing but godlike thoughts and ideas enter your deeper mind.

Some people program their subconscious to receive wisdom and guidance. They have repeated to themselves over and over again: "Infinite Intelligence guides me. Whatever I do will be right. Right action is mine." Morning, noon, and night they reiterate these truths and activate the principle of right action and guidance from a universal or infinite standpoint. Many of them develop the Midas touch and create great prosperity in their lives.

Some people wear an amulet such as a cross, a saint's medal, or other religious symbol to constantly remind them of God. However, you don't need such a talisman or charm. The important thing is to carry the truth of God in your soul. Then you're in communion with God and can communicate with Him instantaneously. You can remind yourself: *My God shall supply all my need according to His riches and glory. In quietness and in confidence shall be my strength.*

You must eat the apple before it enters your bloodstream. Likewise, you have to absorb and digest these truths. As you regularly go within and remind yourself of these truths, gradually you begin to become convinced that there is only One Power. It will become a philosophical absolute in your mind that the "I AM" within you is the only God there is. It is All-Powerful and All-Wise. Here are some great truths:

> *God gives us richly all things to enjoy. With God all things are possible. Before they call I will answer. While they are yet speaking, I will hear. According to your faith be it done unto thee. All things are possible to him that believes. He shall call upon me and I will answer him. I will be with him in trouble. I will deliver him, and honor him. With long life will I satisfy him and show him my salvation. All things are ready if the mind were so. The Lord is my light and my salvation; whom shall I fear? The Lord is the strength of my life; of whom shall I be afraid? Ask and it shall be given you; seek and ye shall find; knock and it shall be opened unto you.*

The Infinite Intelligence of your subconscious mind always responds directly to your conscious thinking. If you ask for bread, you won't receive a stone. You must ask believing that you are to receive. You must reach a point of acceptance in your mind, an unqualified and undisputed state of agreement. This contemplation should be accompanied by a feeling of joy and restfulness in foreseeing the certain accomplishment of your desire. For example, the architect visualizes the type of building he wants built. He sees it as he desires it to be completed and draws his ideas on paper. His imagery and thought processes become a mold from which the building will emerge, whether beautiful or ugly. Eventually the contractor and construction workers gather the essential materials and work until the building is finished, conforming perfectly to the mental patterns of the architect.

You can use the visualization technique, too. If a loved one is ill, quiet the wheels of your mind, then picture the loved one as whole and perfect. Hear that loved one telling you that the miracle of God has happened and that they have never felt better in their life. See the light in their eyes and see them smile. You don't visualize them in the hospital, but at home doing the things they love to do—radiant, happy, and free. You build up that image in your mind. This is prayer. Gradually, the images of your healthy loved one will sink into your deeper mind and wonders will unfold.

Affirm boldly:

I realize that my way is God's way, and all God's ways are pleasantness, and all His paths are peace. I place myself under God's guidance and know that the Almighty Power is guiding me now. The Holy Spirit goes before me, making straight, joyous, and glorious my way. My highway from now on is the royal road of the ancients. It's the middle path of Buddha. It's the straight and narrow gate of Jesus. It's the road to Mecca. My highway is the King's Highway, for I am a king over all my thoughts, feelings, and emotions. These thoughts are messengers of love, peace, light, and beauty that go before me today and every day. While driving a car or riding on a train, bus, or airplane, I realize that God's love is always around me. I am protected by the invisible armor of God and travel from point to point freely, joyously, and lovingly. Divine love fills my soul and Divine peace floods my mind. God is guiding me now, and the light of God illumines my pathway. I know that there is a perfect law of supply and demand and that I am instantly in touch with everything I need.

In a Nutshell

In order to understand how you can create wealth through the power of your subconscious mind, it's important to know how this phenomenon works. The subconscious mind reacts according to our habitual thinking and imagery. As we sow, so shall we reap. What we impress on our subconscious is expressed. If we think "poor" thoughts, we will always be poor. If we think "prosperous" thoughts, we will prosper. We should, therefore, feed our subconscious mind with life-giving patterns.

Many of us were conditioned negatively when we were young and highly impressionable. We must take steps to convert these false suggestions to positive thoughts. There's a right way to program the subconscious mind. Every morning of your life you can sit quietly, get relaxed, and affirm as follows:

Divine law and order govern my life. Divine right action reigns supreme. Divine success is mine. Divine harmony is mine. Divine peace fills my soul. Divine love saturates my whole being and goes before me today and every day, making straight, joyous, and glorious my way.

⊶✛⊷ ⊶✛⊷ ⊶✛⊷

Chapter Four

---·•·---

The Wonderful Power of Decision

*A*ll successful men and women possess one outstanding char-acteristic: their ability to make prompt decisions and to persist in carrying those decisions through to completion. A distin-guished industrialist once told me that in his 50 years of experience in dealing with men and women in the commercial and industrial fields, he found that all those who failed had one characteristic in common: They hesitated to make decisions. They vacillated and waited. Furthermore, when they *did* make decisions, they weren't persistent in adhering to them.

I received a letter from a young member of my congregation that illustrates the power of decision. He had made a clear-cut choice in his mind, knowing that the Almighty Power would back up that decision. He wanted a Volkswagen automobile. He wrote:

> I came to a decision to purchase a car. I didn't have the required amount of money but trusted my deeper mind. I dis-missed the problem from my mind, knowing my subconscious had the answer. A few days later, a friend asked me if I would go to the fair, and I decided to go on Sunday. A car was being given away that night, and I had a 35,000-to-1 chance of winning. My name was selected, and I won my dream car—a Volkswagen. I know the reason I got the car was my trust and faith in my deeper mind to solve the problem of a car, for a car is an idea. As I

continue to use the truths of the Infinite, my life is now in complete harmony. I would like to thank you for opening my eyes to the Supreme Power. Hearing you each Sunday gives me what I need to go through the week. Your thoughts and words are giving me and my family a better life.

I know another young woman who discovered that it's never too late to start making decisions and to live your own life in a wonderful way. When I first met her, she told me that she felt lonesome, baffled, and frustrated because she couldn't decide whether she should marry. Can you imagine that? Her mother was very domineering and objected to every man she was interested in. This young woman had lost all initiative and power of decision, which resulted in loneliness and misery. In other words, she put herself in a house of bondage.

At my suggestion, she began to make one decision after another, whereas previously her mother had made all decisions for her. She decided to purchase her own clothes, get an apartment for herself—and paint and furnish it the way she wanted it—without asking anybody's opinion. She chose to take up dancing, swimming, and golf. She got into the habit of making all decisions for herself and finally decided to marry a wonderful man without consulting her mother or anybody else, following the dictates of her own heart.

It's never too late to bring order to a disordered mind or disordered affairs by making logical decisions and following through on them. I counseled another young woman who transformed her life through the power of decision. Betty L. was 26 years old and living in her parents' home. However, she had a good job and was earning an income adequate to support herself nicely. She told me, "I'm so miserable and unhappy. I want to move to my own apartment, but my parents won't let me. They won't even let me redecorate my room. My entire family says I'm wrong. I'm so undecided. Doesn't God want me to be happy?"

I pointed out to her that she *had* made a decision: She had chosen not to decide. I told Betty that she was blessed with a mind of her own and that it was up to her to resolve to be independent, happy, and prosperous.

She lost no time in determining what she wanted. She made her move and opened up an entirely new world. She wrote to me some months later to inform me that her family had been angry at first, but now is reconciled to her independence. "For the first time in my life, I'm excited and happy. I can hardly believe it," she said.

The following letter shows a woman's faith in her own mental processes and ability to make a decision and stick to it, knowing that her mind is one with the Infinite Mind—for there's only one mind common to all people. She wrote:

> A few years ago I had a serious automobile accident. The doctor said that he'd never seen a neck and back broken in so many places, and he doubted I would live. However, I resolved that I would live and be healed by the Power of the Infinite. I knew all the power of the godhead would respond to my decision, as I heard you say many times that "it is done unto you according to your decision." I asked for prayer ministry, and I claimed frequently that the Infinite Healing Presence was making me whole and perfect—and a marvelous healing followed. I had been told that I would have to wear a body and neck brace for several months, and perhaps a year. I wore the brace only a few weeks, and there's nothing wrong with my neck and back now. My heart is full of gratitude. I know it is done unto you according to your decision. I decided to be healed, and the Infinite Healing Presence responded accordingly.

The power of decision is as important in the practice of business as in the practice of healing. I know a prominent pharmacist who has evolved a wonderful technique for making right decisions and receiving answers to problems, by using the Infinite Power within him. As I was talking with him one day, he mentioned that in his business, making decisions is often confusing and difficult, but that he had mastered what he believes to be the ideal method of arriving at the right decision and the correct thing to do. He said: "I dwell on the fact that God, or Infinite Intelligence, dwells within me, and I focus all my attention on the Infinite Presence within me. I imagine that the Infinite is answering me. I relax and let go completely, and feel myself surrounded by the love and the light of the Infinite. I also feel myself immersed in God's quietness and stillness. As clear as crystal, the answer pops into my mind, and it's always right."

Whenever you are wondering what to do or say, or what decision to make, sit quietly and affirm this truth:

Whatever I need to know comes to me from the Infinite Presence within. Infinite Intelligence is operating through me, revealing to me what I need to know. I radiate love, peace, and goodwill to all humankind in thought, word, and deed. I know that what I send out comes back to me a thousandfold. God in me knows the answer. The perfect answer is made known to me now, for God is the eternal now. Now is the day of salvation, and now is the accepted time. Divine Wisdom makes all decisions through me, and there is only right action and right decision taking place in my life. I wrap myself in the mantle of that Infinite ocean of love, and I know Divine right decision is mine now. I am at peace. I walk in the light, full of faith and confidence, and trust in the only Power there is. I recognize the lead that comes into my conscious, reasoning mind. It is impossible for me to miss it. God speaks to me in peace, not in confusion. Thank you, Father, for the answer now.

This is a wonderful prayer that I have given to thousands of men and women for guidance in making decisions. They have received marvelous results and have been blessed in all their choices. Say it slowly, quietly, reverently, and with feeling. Do this about three times in a relaxed, peaceful mood, and you will receive the Divine impulse. You will experience the inner silent knowing of the soul. Sometimes the answer comes as an inner feeling of certitude, a predominant hunch, or a spontaneous idea that comes up clearly in your mind like bread pops out of the toaster. Intuitively you will recognize the right answer and the best decision to make. Pray, realizing that there's an Infinite Intelligence that responds to you. *When you call upon It, It answers you. Ask and ye shall receive. Seek and ye shall find. Knock and it shall be opened to you. If you ask for bread, you will not receive a stone.*

Logical decisions are always based upon this Infinite Wisdom that guides the planets on their course and causes the sun to shine. I worked with a young woman who tapped into the power of Infinite Wisdom to launch a new career. This woman, who worked for a department store in Los Angeles, had been interested in the stock market for many years and had become a very successful investor. She took a night course that qualified her for employment in a brokerage house. She had numerous interviews but was unable to get a job in her new chosen field because, as she believed, of her gender. She said to me, "They just don't want women."

I suggested that she come to a decision and affirm boldly: "I am now employed in a brokerage firm, earning a marvelous income." I explained to her that the minute she came to a decision in her mind and persisted in that decision, her subconscious mind would respond and open up the way by revealing the perfect plan for fulfillment of her ideal. I also instructed her to follow the lead that would come to her conscious, reasoning mind.

The sequel, of course, is interesting. A strong urge came to her to advertise in the local newspaper, offering to work for free for two months and pointing out that she had a large circle of friends who could be potential customers. She received immediate offers from three firms and happily accepted one of them. This anecdote shows that you must have faith in your ability to decide. When you come to a clear-cut decision, backed by faith in the power of your subconscious mind, wonders will happen in your life and you will banish all frustration.

People who fear making decisions are actually refusing to recognize their own Divinity, for it's your Divine right to make choices. Accept your Divinity and your responsibility to make decisions for yourself now. You can decide to be healthy, happy, prosperous, and successful because you have dominion over your world. Your subconscious mind is subject to the decrees of your conscious mind, and whatever you decree shall come to pass. Whatever you sow in your subconscious mind, you shall reap on the screen of space as form, experience, and conditions. It's therefore wise to choose thoughts that are true, lovely, pure, and just.

The law of your subconscious mind is as consistent as any law of nature. If you put your hand on a hot stove, you will suffer a burn. If you jump off the roof of a high building, the law of gravity will cause you to plummet toward your death. Similarly, if you dwell on thoughts of lack and limitation, you create more misery in your life, but if you focus on drawing wealth and opportunity to you, you will lead a life of prosperity. It's foolish to try to act against the laws of nature, because they're immutable.

According to the law of the subconscious, if you don't make a clear decision, by default you decide to take what comes from the mass mind in which we're all immersed—and it's a very negative mind, full of fear, hate, and jealousy. The mass mind believes in tragedies and misfortunes of all kinds. It's therefore illogical and unwise to be indecisive. If you refuse to make a decision, you let circumstances and conditions—or your mother-in-law or boyfriend—make a decision for you.

You're an individual with the capacity to decide, and you're here to choose—to mold and fashion your own destiny. The Infinite Power backs up all of your decisions. When you allow someone to make your decisions, you rob yourself of your own initiative and experience. It's wrong to say, "I will let God decide for me." When you say that, you mean a God outside of yourself, someone up in the sky somewhere. The only way God, or Infinite Intelligence, will work for you is *through* you—through your own thought, your own imagery, and your own decision. The God Presence is within your subconscious depths, and you are here to use it.

Learn to make decisions. Start now. When you are seven or eight years of age, you should learn to make decisions to some degree—with supervision, of course. But by the time you're an adult, you should certainly make your own decisions, move out of your parents' home, establish your own apartment, roll up your sleeves, and get busy. Learn to exercise your initiative.

If you need to make a decision, affirm to yourself, "I believe in my power, my ability, and the integrity of my own mental and spiritual processes. I know my desire is to do the right thing. Infinite Wisdom is making all decisions through me, leading to right action and beneficial outcomes."

It's possible to reverse even the most destructive of decisions. For example, a confirmed alcoholic once told me that he couldn't stop drinking. He said, "I have to drink. I can't stop. It's a compulsive act." I explained to him that all the power of the Infinite was behind his decision to drink, but that he could change this decision. At my suggestion, he declared solemnly for about ten minutes: "I have come to a definite conclusion in my mind, and my decision is that I am free from this curse of alcoholism. Through the Infinite Power that backs up this decision, I am completely free. I have peace of mind and sobriety, and I give thanks to the Infinite now."

This man hasn't touched any intoxicating beverages for over five years and is completely free of the habit. He's a new man. When he made a decision, he meant it. The power was not in the bottle; the power was within him. The Power of the Infinite is also behind all of your decisions. *Choose this day whom you will serve.*

There's but One Power—the Infinite Intelligence that can cast light on any problem. All that's required is that you come to a clear-cut decision in your mind. You create darkness when you say, "I'm stymied. I'm blocked. There's no way out." That's a foolish decision. The Infinite knows the way. By decreeing that your situation is hopeless, you're foolishly affirming that Infinite Intelligence doesn't know the way out—and as you believe, it is done unto you. You'll live in the darkness and confusion created by your ignorance of the law and failure to come to the right decision.

Last year I counseled a man who overcame the darkness in his mind. He had gone bankrupt a short time previously and had developed ulcers and high blood pressure. He was, as he said, "in a mess." He believed that he was cursed and that God was punishing him for his past sins. These were false beliefs in his mind.

I explained to him that as long as he believed that he was jinxed, he would suffer—for the simple reason that one's beliefs take form as experiences, conditions, and events. I told him that he had to come to a clear-cut decision in his mind that there is only One Power and that this Power is harmony, healing, and love.

He made this decision and created this meditation:

> *There is but One Creator, One Presence, One Power. This Power is within me as my mind and spirit. This Presence moves through me as harmony, health, and peace. I think, speak, and act from the standpoint of Infinite Intelligence. I know that thoughts are things. What I feel, I attract; what I imagine, I become. I constantly dwell on these truths. I have come to a clear-cut decision that Divine right action governs my life. Divine law and order reign supreme and operate in all phases of my life. Divine guidance is mine. Divine success is mine. Divine prosperity is mine. Divine love fills my soul. Divine wisdom governs all my transactions. Whenever fear or worry comes into my mind, I affirm immediately: "God is guiding me now" or "God knows the answer." I make a habit of this, and I know miracles are happening in my life.*

He prayed out loud in this manner five or six times daily. At the end of a month, his health was restored and he was chosen as a partner in a growing business. His whole life had been transformed. He came to a decision that the One Power moved in his life as harmony, health, and peace and that nothing opposed or thwarted it. This new decision in his mind compelled him to express the riches of life.

Another woman I know used the power of decision to heal a financial situation. She came to visit me, visibly upset. She had invested a considerable sum in a venture, with the agreement that she would pay an additional amount by a certain date. As the payment date neared, she realized that she couldn't raise the money and would lose her entire investment. She had done all that she could to honor her obligation, but still didn't have the money. She was about to succumb to panic when her strong faith in God reasserted itself. She came to a definite, clear-cut decision that she would reject any fearful or destructive thoughts about the matter that came to her. She worked out a simple prayer: "I know that You know the answer and that You will show me the way. Thank You for bringing it about now."

She told me later, "I held on to that prayer as though my life depended on it. For days I recited it to myself, reiterating it silently and quietly. I even sang it aloud when I was by myself."

Very soon she noticed that her sense of panic and desperation had eased; she felt calmer, even though outwardly nothing had changed. The day arrived when she no longer had any inclination to worry and felt lighthearted about things. She knew that her prayer was being answered. As it turned out, an associate mentioned her situation to a friend with enormous sums of money to invest. This friend was very interested in her business venture and loaned her the needed money. What she had been seeking had been seeking her.

Our decisions determine what is done unto us. Enthrone in your mind Divine ideas of good—and watch the wonders that unfold as you pray. Say yes to all ideas and truths that heal, bless, inspire, elevate, and dignify your soul. Say no to all negative thoughts—to anything that would instill fear in your mind and that would drag you down. Reject any suggestion that doesn't give you more confidence and more faith in yourself.

Don't procrastinate in making decisions. Procrastination is the thief of time; and you'll become neurotic, frustrated, and unhappy. It's far better to do something right now than nothing. In making a decision, you set Spirit in motion to begin to manifest your desires. If you remain indecisive, you block the flow of good into your life.

For example, a few years ago I talked with a man in a hotel. He was 90 years old and was on crutches. We talked for quite a while, and he said, "You know, when I was younger, I wanted to take my wife on a trip around the world, but I postponed it. I said, 'I'll wait until my daughter grows up and gets married.' Now my wife is dead and I'm crippled with arthritis and I'll never realize that dream."

This man didn't give himself or his wife the joy of that trip. He refused to come to a decision. He postponed his dream, waiting until his daughter grew up and got married, and still didn't go—all of which is nonsense. Your good is right now. Don't wait for anything. Do it now. A trip around the world has nothing to do with your daughter getting married or remaining single—nothing at all to do with it. It has to do with you. Make up your mind and come to a clear-cut decision. If your motivation is right, that decision is right. It's God in action, right now.

Tom Monaghan is a man who didn't shirk making decisions. He created and grew Domino's Pizza from a one-store pizza parlor to an international, billion-dollar franchise over a period of about 35 years. In 1989 he decided to sell his hugely successful company to concentrate instead on doing philanthropic work. However, after the company that purchased the chain nearly drove it into bankruptcy, Monaghan made the tough decision to put aside his chosen activities and save Domino's. It took much hard work and persistence to first rebuild and then expand the organization, but Monaghan had developed the necessary determination early in his life. He had overcome a childhood of deprivation, poverty, and abuse to become a great entrepreneur. Now he once again mobilized all his efforts to not only return Domino's to its original prominence, but to expand the chain to more than 6,000 stores.

Once the chain was back on its feet, Monaghan faced a new and even more serious challenge. Domino's had built its major promotion on their guarantee of fast delivery. They guaranteed that customers would get their pizza within 30 minutes of ordering. This led to a series of lawsuits from people who had been involved in automobile accidents that they claimed were caused by Domino's delivery drivers speeding to make the 30-minute deadline.

Despite this financial catastrophe, Monaghan refused to give up. He plowed more money, time, and energy into the company and brought it back once again. Through his persistence and positive attitude, he forged ahead and inspired his team with the winning spirit that has made Domino's a leader in its industry.

When you pray for guidance and you want to make a decision, say: "Infinite Intelligence is guiding me. There is right action in my life. There is an Overshadowing Presence in which I live, move, and have my being. It opens up the door for me. I follow the lead that comes to me clearly. I turn it over now to the deeper mind, and I go on about my business."

The first intuitive impulse that comes to you is usually the right answer. That impulse comes from your subconscious mind. The answers come out of the depths of Infinite Mind. It's that inner silent knowing of the soul. You don't argue with it or talk to your relatives about it. If you do, you'll have 20 thoughts in your mind.

I have talked to hundreds of women who ignored their intuitive impulse and entered into unhappy marriages. They say, "I knew as I was walking up the aisle to marry that man that I shouldn't do it." That lingering feeling was a sort of hunch from the Life Principle seeking to protect them. Unfortunately, they ignored it and eventually had to get a divorce.

When you want to get married, come to a decision and say, "Infinite Intelligence attracts to me the right person who harmonizes with me in every way. The deeper currents of my mind bring both of us together." Trust the Infinite Intelligence. Don't ask your mother or grandmother whether you should marry the man or woman, because you're then denying your Divinity. You're saying, "Look, I can't choose," which, of course, you can. That's your prerogative.

The decision of whether to divorce is as important as the question of whether to marry. I have seen couples live together in hate and resentment for many years rather than get a divorce. They said that they were staying together for the sake of the children.

However, children grow up in the image and the likeness of the dominant mental and emotional climate of the home. The children of unhappy parents often become delinquents; are sick all the time; and experience a great deal of resentment, hostility, and rage. Realize that it's far more decent, honorable, and Godlike to choose to dissolve the marriage than to contaminate the minds of all those about you.

Of course, before making a decision, it's important to gather your facts and clear your mind. Avoid being swept away by negative emotions. I talked with a man who let his emotions get the best of him. Full of bitterness and hostility, he got mad at the boss, told him off, and quit in a huff. He took another job and said to me, "I have more problems in this job than I had in the previous job." You see, he had made a decision on the basis of anger, resentment, and hostility—his emotions. He was carried away by his emotions. He realized that his decision was wrong.

Instead of acting rashly, gather all the data that you can about your situation. Assemble the facts and consider your options and ask yourself which course seems most reasonable. Study the pros and cons. Don't grit your teeth and clench your fists. Always remember that if your motivation is positive and you're praying for guidance and right action, your decision will be good.

In making a decision, ask yourself if your choice serves others as well as yourself. If you're trying to hoodwink or cheat someone, your decision will be wrong—and to hurt another is to hurt yourself. So ask yourself if your decision is based upon the golden rule and the law of love. Love is wishing for everyone what you wish for yourself. When you love another, you love to see the other become and express all that they long to become and express.

Don't worry about making mistakes. Everybody makes mistakes. When you went to school, didn't you make hundreds of them? That's why you had an eraser on the end of your pencil. Everybody, including your mother and father, knew you'd make mistakes. You can always correct your course. If you're going to San Francisco and discover you're on the wrong road, you change your course and get on the right one. You don't get upset or berate yourself for the mistake but continue on your journey. As you continue to make decisions, you enjoy the zest and thrill of discovery.

The angels watch over you and guide you in your decisions. Angels are the intelligence, the wisdom, and the creative ideas that well up within you. You're guided to your true place, to do the right thing, for the highest and best moves through you. Claim that you're under the protection of the Almighty: "I will say of the Lord, He is my refuge and my fortress. My God, in Him will I trust." Isn't that a wonderful prayer for guidance and right action?

When you go to sleep at night, say: "Infinite Intelligence reveals the right answer or decision to me. When I awaken in the morning, the first thought I have will be the answer." Then observe the first thought you have in the morning. Don't go around pacing the floor and wondering about it. The answer will come to you. You're claiming Divine law and order in your life, which means that the law of harmony, beauty, love, peace, and abundance—rather than the chaos and dogmas of mass mind—is operating in your subconscious. It also means that you're expressing yourself at your highest level. You are releasing your talents in a wonderful way. According to Divine law and order, you also receive marvelous compensation. When you're able to do what you want to do when you want to do it, you're truly rich.

Sometimes people ask me: "Is it right for me to pray for wealth? Is it right for me to pray for success? Maybe God doesn't want me to succeed." That is stupidity. It's jungle philosophy. Or someone might ask: "Does God want me to sing?" Well, if God gave you a voice, He wants you to sing. If you are able to sing and that talent is within you, go ahead and sing. God will sing through you. God is the only Presence and Power. If you have the desire to paint, go ahead and paint. Whether you want to be a veterinarian, a chemist, or a musician, go ahead and follow the lead that comes to you.

People also sometimes ask me: "Is it right to pray for a car?" What is a car? An idea in the mind of God—and that's all a car is. It's the spirit of God made manifest. It's God outside your door taking the form of a car. It's nothing but God—so of course it's fine to pray for a car.

These kinds of questions are based on superstition, ignorance, and fear. If you pray for guidance, you will overcome this ignorance about God and how He manifests in the material world. The spirit of truth will lead you to all truth. Say: "God is guiding me now. Right action reigns supreme. The spirit of truth leads me to all truth." You've come to a marvelous decision. If you pray for prosperity, success, achievement, and victory, come to a decision and say: "Prosperity is mine now. I'm going to be wealthy. I'm going to have all the wealth that I need to do what I want to do when I want to do it"—and your subconscious will respond.

If you're praying for prosperity and success and you're jealous of others or of their promotion, possessions, or wealth, then resentment and envy blocks your good and inhibits your growth, and of course, interferes with your own prosperity—you're inhibiting the flow of the Infinite ocean of riches through you. Wish, therefore, for everyone what you wish for yourself. For love is the fulfilling of the law. Say: "From the depths of my heart, I wish for every person in the world the riches of the Infinite: health, happiness, peace, and all the blessings of life." Then watch how vitality and riches flow to you.

If you're down on yourself, full of regrets and remorse, you also inhibit the flow of good toward you. You're simply using the power of the Infinite against yourself. Remember that the Infinite and Absolute cannot punish you. You punish yourself through your negative, destructive thinking—through your misuse of law. You won't get a healing with that attitude of mind. Instead, exalt God and give Him your allegiance and devotion. Put your faith in the One Power that gives you life, breath, and all things.

You're the temple of the Living God and the kingdom of God is within you. Therefore, the Infinite Wisdom and Power is within you. If you were God, what decision would you make? You'd make a decision based on right action, harmony, peace, love, and goodwill, wouldn't you? You would begin to think, speak, and act from the standpoint of the Infinite Center. You wouldn't make any decisions from the standpoint of some old theologian or of your grandmother. You'd say, "There is a Guiding Principle within me, and I'm going to make decisions according to that Guiding Principle, which is absolute harmony and absolute peace."

God wants you to be happy, and your decision should be to lead a full and joyous life. God richly gave you all things to enjoy. God created you so you might have life and have it more abundantly. You're here to glorify God and enjoy Him forever. Until now you've asked for nothing; now ask that your joy might be full. In God there's fullness of joy; in Him there's no darkness at all.

The power and the wisdom of the Infinite always sends you messages about how to attain greater happiness and wealth if you go within and ask. For example, one of my congregants prayed about an investment recently in Nevada. He said: "Infinite Intelligence is guiding me. It reveals to me and to my wife the right thing to do regarding this investment." Then he had a dream in the middle of the night in which he saw the leaders of the company in which he had planned to invest in prison with guards around them and a guard with a gun at the door. He woke up and knew that he was dealing with con men who had served time. Had he invested, he would have lost everything.

You have to come to a decision that there is a Guiding Principle within you, and wonders will happen in your life. When you have what you consider a difficult decision to make, or when you fail to see the solution to your problem, begin at once to think constructively about it. If you are fearful and worried, you're not really thinking. True thinking is free from fear. Quiet the mind, still the body. Tell your body to relax; it has to obey you. Your body has no volition, initiative, or self-conscious intelligence. Your body is an emotional disk that records your beliefs and impressions. Focus your thought on the solution to your problem. Get all the information you can and think about how happy you would be about the perfect solution. If you're going to sleep, then drop off to sleep contemplating the answer. When you awaken, if you don't have the answer, get busy doing something else. When you are preoccupied with something else, the answer will come into your mind easily and effortlessly.

For example, a man lost a valuable ring, which was an heirloom. He looked everywhere for it but couldn't find it. At night he offered a prayer to his subconscious for an answer to arrive in his sleep. He said: "You know all things. You are all wise. You are omnipresent. You know where that ring is. You are now revealing to me where it is." In the morning he awoke suddenly with the words ringing in his ear: "Ask Robert." Robert was his son. The man asked Robert about the ring, and he said, "Oh, yes. I picked it up in the yard while I was playing with the boys. I put it on the desk in my room. I didn't think it was worth anything, so I didn't say anything about it."

When you call upon It, It will answer you; it will be with you in trouble; it will set you On High, because you have known its name. And in quietness and in confidence shall be your strength.

In a Nutshell

The power to decide is a person's foremost quality. God has bequeathed you with the capacity to choose and to initiate. It's your Divine right to choose and to make decisions. You can decide to be healthy, happy, prosperous, and successful because you have dominion over your world. Your subconscious mind is subject to the decrees of your conscious mind, and whatever you decree shall come to pass.

When you refuse to make decisions for yourself, you're actually rejecting your Divinity, thinking from the standpoint of weakness and inferiority just like a slave and an underling. Make decisions and acknowledge your Divinity.

Choose whatever is true, lovely, just, pure, and honest. Decide to enthrone these thoughts in your mind, and stick to that decision. It's logical for you to choose good thoughts, since only good can follow. It's illogical for you to choose evil thoughts and to still expect good, because seeds, or thoughts, grow after their kind.

When you pray for guidance and you want to make a decision, say: "Infinite Intelligence is guiding me. There is right action in my life. There is an Overshadowing Presence in which I live, move, and have my being. It opens up the door for me."

If you're praying for prosperity, success, and achievement but are jealous of others—of their promotion, possessions, or money—that negative feeling blocks your good, inhibits your growth, and of course, interferes with your own prosperity.

Your decision should be to lead a full and happy life. God richly gave you all things to enjoy. God created you so that you might have life and have it more abundantly.

※✝※ ※✝※ ※✝※

Chapter Five

The Wonders of a Disciplined Imagination

*I*magination is the genesis of all action. It's the mighty instrument used by scientists, artists, inventors, architects, and mystics. To imagine is to conceive an idea and to impress it on your subconscious mind. Whatever is impressed on the subconscious is expressed on the screen of space as form, experience, and event. If you wish to be successful, you must first imagine yourself as successful. If you wish to be wealthy, you must first imagine yourself as wealthy. When the world says, "It's impossible, it can't be done," the person with imagination says, "It's already done." Imagination is the workshop of God, where ideas and desires are transformed and manifested in our daily lives. As we imagine, so we will become, achieve, and experience.

I know a great industrialist who truly cultivated his imagination and focused on his vision of running a hugely successful business until his dream became reality. He told me, "I used to dream of running a large corporation with branches all over the country." He added that he regularly and systematically pictured in his mind the giant offices, factories, and stores, knowing that through the power of the mind he could weave the fabric out of which his dreams would be clothed. He prospered and began to attract the ideas, personnel, friends, money, and everything else needed for the fulfillment of his dream. I particularly liked one comment that he made: "It's just as easy to imagine yourself as successful as it is to imagine failure—and it's far more interesting."

Consider for a moment that all we see and find useful and practical in our lives has come forth from the imaginative faculties of men and women: the clothing we wear, the cars we drive, the seats upon which we rest, the houses in which we live, and more. All the great works of art are the products of inspired imagination. The painting of the beautiful Madonna first existed in the mind of the disciplined artist. It's the imagination that leads humankind onward and Godward.

People have been using the power of imagination since the earliest times. Archaeologists tell us that prehistoric cave dwellers carved pictures on cave walls of the animals and fish that they wanted to catch. Why did they do that? Some scientists say that these early people instinctively knew that by picturing (literally) what they wanted, some Power would bring this source of food into their lives so that they could eat. You see, they understood the law of mind—the power of imagination.

In the golden age of Greece, more than 2,500 years ago, the ancient Greeks used the law of mind and imagination. Pregnant women surrounded themselves with beautiful pictures and statues so that their unborn children might receive from their mother's mind images of health, beauty, symmetry, and order. The women would gaze on this lovely art so that their children would be born with these qualities of grace and reason.

Perhaps you have a dream or plan that you'd like to accomplish, but friends, colleagues, and others tell you that it cannot be done, You may even say to yourself: "Who do you think you are? You can't do that. You don't know enough and you don't have the right contacts." Well, in fact, you *do* have everything you need to accomplish your goal. The "right contact" is the God Presence within you that gave you your idea. This God Presence can bring your dream to fruition in Divine order, through Divine love.

The way to handle the opposition in your mind is to detach your attention from the evidence of the senses and the appearance of things and begin to think clearly and with interest about what you want. When your mind is engaged on your objective, you're using the creative law of your mind, and your dream will be fulfilled.

In order to receive, you must first conceive or picture your desire. There's an old fable that illustrates this concept. There was a Persian prince who had a crooked back and couldn't stand up straight. He hired a skillful sculptor to make a statue of himself—true to his likeness in all ways—but with his back as straight as an arrow. "I wish to see myself as I ought to be and as God wants me to be," the prince said. Well, the sculptor completed the statue and the prince placed it in a secret corner of his garden. Two or three times every day, regularly and systematically, he would go into his garden and meditate upon the statue, particularly the straightness of the spine. As the months passed, people began to say, "The prince's back is no longer crooked. He stands up straight like a nobleman." The fable says that the prince went out into the garden, and behold—it was true—his back was as straight as the statue's.

Through your faculty to imagine your desired end result, you have control over any circumstance or condition. If you wish to bring about the realization of any wish, desire, or plan, form a mental picture of fulfillment in your mind. Constantly imagine the reality of your desire. In this way you'll actually compel it into being. Give your attention, love, and devotion to your desire. Exalt it and commit yourself wholeheartedly to its fulfillment. As you continue to do so, all your fearful thoughts will lose their power and disappear from your mind.

I know an actor who used this power of the mind to achieve his desire to become renowned in his profession. He told me that at the beginning of his career he was mediocre. He had small parts but was struggling to make it. However, he used the powers of his subconscious mind. Every night for 15 minutes he imagined himself as a successful actor, masterfully acting in starring roles—exalting the power of the Spirit within him. He regularly and systematically visualized his success, creating a pattern in his subconscious mind that resulted in his reaching the heights of his profession. He knew that the power of the Almighty would back him up.

Robbie Wright, a member of my radio staff, also used the law of mind and recently won a prize in a drag race. He said that he "psyched himself up" before the race. He imagined himself winning and receiving congratulations from his friends and brother. He felt a Supreme Power controlling him in the race—that Power was responding to the image in his mind of victory and triumph.

You can use your imagination in two ways: to achieve success or to attract failure. If you look at the top of a mountain and say, "I'm going to go there," you will. But if you say, "I'm old, I might get blisters, it's too difficult," you won't get to the top of the mountain. Imagination can carry you to tremendous heights or carry you to the lowest depths. Someone who constantly fails has an image of defeat in his mind. Someone who is chronically ill and always complaining carries an image of ill health and weakness. If a businessman continually imagines that bankruptcy is in his future, this will come to pass. You can imagine sickness and failure, but it's foolish to do so.

Imagination is more powerful than discipline or self-coercion in overcoming bad habits. For example, alcoholics know that if they rely on sheer willpower to give up alcohol, it drives them further to drink. But when they contemplate sobriety and peace of mind and imagine themselves healthy and doing what they love to do—knowing that an Almighty Power is backing up their mental picture—they free themselves of the habit and are healed.

The imagination is also a supreme tool for overcoming physical illness. Dr. Carl Simonton, a cancer specialist, has taught many patients how to use visualization and meditation to overcome cancer. He describes the first patient he treated at Travis Air Force Base. The patient was a nonsmoker who had a tumor on the roof of his mouth and another, larger tumor in the back of his throat. He could no longer eat and had lost a great deal of weight. According to the medical field, he had about a 5 to 10 percent chance of being cured of both cancers. However, Dr. Simonton believes that the power of the mind can be used to influence a person's ability to survive serious disease and worked with him to tap into this source of natural healing. He taught the patient to relax and visualize the cancer responding to his radiation treatment, returning to perfect health, with ideally functioning cells. He did this visualization three times every day, and the results were truly amazing. Today he no longer has any evidence of cancer in his body. Dr. Simonton provides further insight into this amazing healing:

> I should emphasize that he was an extremely positive patient. He was also very cooperative, and after one week of treatment the tumor was beginning to shrink. After four weeks of treatment the ulceration had no growth evidence of tumor, and so it was doing essentially the same thing—showing a very dramatic response. It was generally outside my experience to get such dramatic response in two separate tumors in such a short time. After one month there was one small ulceration healing nicely; and about ten weeks after treatment the roof of his mouth was essentially normal in appearance. The truly beautiful thing was that the lesion in the throat showed the same response as the one in the mouth, and on routine examination it was impossible to tell where the throat tumor had been. Only three months after he had been taken off flying status, this man had unanimous clearance to go back on flying status and resume his profession.

Now I grant you that there are some people who don't want to get well. They rejoice in their misery, enjoying getting attention and sympathy for their plight. They talk about their illness incessantly and thereby perpetuate it. However, God's intention for you is that you express yourself at the highest level, enjoying perfect health.

In your journey through life, however difficult it may be, remember that there's a holy place within you—the sanctuary of

God—where you can feel your kinship with the One Who Forever Is. Realize that the Invisible Presence within you will lead you and assist you in the realization of your dream. Through the power of your imagination, you can release the flower of love and beauty from your heart.

If you visualize your desired outcome regularly and systematically, the Universe will move on your behalf to fulfill your desire. For example, some years ago I met a young man who had been drafted into the Army and was bemoaning the fact that his plan to become a doctor had been thwarted. I told him: "Picture yourself as a doctor. You have a diploma from a fine medical school telling that you are now a physician and surgeon. You have a successful practice treating patients. Use the law of your mind and visualize your desired result." I explained the laws of his mind to him in five minutes, and he quickly understood. He began to imagine his life as a doctor, and sometime later the Army sent him to medical school. Today he's a doctor.

Your imagination, when disciplined, enables you to rise above all limitations. You can imagine anything. You can imagine your friend who is poor living in the lap of luxury. You can witness his face light up with joy, watch his expression change, and see a broad smile cross his lips. You can hear him tell you what you want to hear. You can see him exactly as you wish—radiant, happy, prosperous, and successful. You can imagine abundance where there is lack, peace where there is discord, and health where there is sickness.

You can also use the power of the imagination to help people heal who are far away. Distance is no barrier to the power of the mind. Suppose your mother is sick in the hospital in another state. If you know the law of mind, you realize that the healing power of God is flowing through your mom and that Divine love is healing, guiding, and watching over her. Divine love is also guiding the doctors and nurses and all who minister to her. This is what you can affirm. Visualize her in front of you, telling you about the miracle of God that is happening in her life, how she is vital and alive, bubbling over with enthusiasm. She's telling you what you long to hear. You can see her as clearly as if she were present. Then you are really praying and using the law of mind.

When doing this affirmation, it's important that you don't dwell on your mother's illness or imagine her in the hospital. If you affirm one thing but imagine another, you won't get your desired results because your image has to agree with your affirmation. Nothing could be simpler than that. Often I say that 99 percent of people don't know how to pray. Oh, yes, they say wonderful prayers, but in their mind they are imagining their relative in the hospital or in jail or in some other difficult situation.

The imagination is a tool that you can use in any area of your life. For example, suppose the teacher says your son is slow in school or has a learning disability. What do you do? First you sit down and relax the body. Say to yourself, "My toes are relaxed. My feet are relaxed. My abdominal muscles are relaxed. My heart and lungs are relaxed. My spine is relaxed. My neck is relaxed. My hands and arms are relaxed. My eyes are relaxed. My whole being is completely relaxed from head to toe." The Almighty Power begins to work through you when you calm your body and mind. If you don't, your prayer will not get results, so relax and believe.

Now imagine your son right in front of you. He's telling you, "Mom, you know I'm getting all A's. The teacher congratulated me." You realize that the Infinite Intelligence flows through your son. The wisdom of God anoints his intellect. He's happy and able to learn easily and effortlessly. This is an example of using directed imagination, a law of the mind. It's very simple.

You can also use the power of imagination to deal with the experience of death. Imagine yourself going to the funeral of a friend. Notice the different emotions you feel as you picture yourself in this particular situation. If you know the law of mind, you can rejoice in the person's new birthday. You can imagine the loved one surrounded by his or her friends in the midst of indescribable beauty in the next dimension of life. You can imagine God's river of peace flowing through the minds and hearts of all those present. You can actually ascend the heavens of your own mind, wherever you are. That's the power of imagination. There's no one buried anywhere, you know. If you think someone is buried, you're identifying with limitation and finality. You're building a cemetery in your own mind.

Through your faculty of imagination, you can also imagine the secrets of nature and history revealed to you. This is what a relative of mine did when we traveled to Ireland together. We came across a round tower, and my relative stood examining it for an hour. He said nothing, seeming to be in a pensive mood. I asked him what he was meditating on, and he said that he was contemplating the age of the stones in the tower. His imagination took him back to the quarries where the stones were first formed. He saw with the interior eye the structure, the geological formation, and the composition of the stones. Finally, he imagined the oneness of the stones with all stones, with all life, and with the whole world.

He realized in his Divine imagination that it was possible to reconstruct the history of the Irish race from looking at the round tower. He was able to see the invisible souls living in the round tower and hear their voices. The whole place became alive to him in his imagination. Through this power, he was able to go back to a time before a round tower was there. In his mind he began to weave a drama of the place from which the stones originated, the people who quarried them, the purpose of the tower, and the history connected with it. He said to me, "I am almost able to feel the touch and hear the sound of steps that vanished thousands of years ago."

If you believe that God is the spiritual power within you, responsive to your thought, and guiding and prospering you in all your ways, you will accomplish great things. Your outlook will be positive, and you will have a joyous expectancy of the best. You will radiate love, peace, and goodwill to everyone in the world and have success in all areas of your life.

A good example of someone who used his imagination to create an extremely successful businesses is Howard Schultz, the chairman of Starbucks Coffee Company. In 1982 Schultz was hired as the director of marketing and operations for Starbucks, then a small coffee distributor with a few retail outlets in Seattle. He was 29 and newly married. About a year later, Schultz visited Italy on a buying trip and noticed how important coffee is to the Italian culture. Typically, the workday starts with a cup of espresso at a coffee bar. Friends and colleagues also meet at these bars for a leisurely cup of coffee at other times throughout the day and early evening. It's a hub of Italian social life.

Schultz visualized creating coffee bars like this in America. It had never been done, but he felt that it could work because of the high quality of Starbucks coffee. Schultz envisioned developing hundreds of Starbucks coffee shops across America, and it became his obsession. He was determined to build a national chain of shops based on the Italian coffee bar, but Starbucks' owners were reluctant. They were in the wholesale coffee-bean business and said they didn't want to get into the restaurant arena.

To implement his goal, Schultz left Starbucks and started his own coffee-bar, Il Giornale. It was an immediate success. Schultz soon opened another in Seattle and a third in Vancouver. In 1987 he bought Starbucks and adopted its name for his enterprise.

Starbucks now has coffee bars in hundreds of cities and has become a household name around the world—an exemplar of American marketing ingenuity. Howard Schultz had a firm conviction about the business he wanted to create and has become one of the wealthiest men in the world. His story is a powerful illustration of the wonderful way the tool of imagination can be used.

If you imagine that you're successful and doing what you love—and don't deny what you affirm—you have to succeed, because the law of mind backs you up. I worked with a high school student who used this law to overcome his problems at school. He told me, "I'm getting very poor grades. My memory is failing, and I don't know what's wrong." The only thing wrong with him was his attitude. I explained the principles of spiritual mind treatment to him, and he began to use affirmative prayer. He began to systematically claim that there was a Spiritual Power within him, that his memory was perfect, and that Infinite Intelligence constantly revealed everything that he needed to know at all times.

He constantly imagines the teachers and his mother congratulating him on his marvelous work and his wonderful grades. As a result, he's now enjoying a greater freedom than he's known for years and is doing extremely well in school. He also radiates goodwill to his teachers and fellow students, which is very, very important.

You can imagine that it's going to be a black day today, that business is going to be very poor, that no customers will come to your store, and that you have no money—and you will experience the results of your negative imagery. It's far better to fill your imagination with vivid thoughts of your desires. A woman I know replaced her dark thoughts about the "poor economy" with thoughts of earning a good profit on the sale of her house. She told me that she had been trying to sell a home that had been bequeathed to her by her father. It was worth half a million dollars. She said, "I'm a widow. I'm all alone, and I want to sell this place. But people don't have that kind of money today. They look at the price and never come back."

I said to her, "Look, this is what you need to do. Stop your nonsense. Walk through this mansion of yours and imagine you're showing it to an imaginary buyer. You're showing him the whole place—the garage, the garden, and everything else—and he's saying, 'I like it. I'm going to take it,' and he's giving you a check for it. You're happy about it and are taking the check to the bank. The banker is saying, 'Congratulations, you've sold your place.' You visualize the entire sales process in your mind because if you don't sell the house in your mind, you'll never sell it—for all transactions take place in the mind."

If the woman tells herself that money is tight, that mortgage rates are high, and that nobody has half a million dollars to buy a house, she will never sell it. Instead, she needs to realize that there are many millionaires and affirm: "Infinite Intelligence attracts to me the buyer who appreciates this home, wants it, and has the money to pay for it." That's the quickest way in the world to sell it.

After she began to regularly and systematically affirm what she wanted, she quickly sold the house for a satisfactory price.

What should you imagine for your life? Well, the Bible tells you to imagine whatever is true, just, lovely, pure, and honest. Imagine conditions and circumstances in life that dignify, elevate, please, and satisfy. Imagine your husband or wife telling you what you long to hear—how much they love and care for you, how they have been promoted at work, how wonderful life is for them with you, and how happy they are. Imagine what you want in rich detail, and don't deny what you affirm.

Keep in mind, however, that you can't use affirmative prayer to force anyone to do your will or make them feel a certain way about you. I receive letters from men and women in different states of the union. They say, "I want this woman to marry me. She pays no attention to me. Will you tell me how to pray and get her?" It's almost unbelievable! I write them and say that I can't imagine any man in the world wanting a woman who doesn't want him, provided the man is in his right mind. If you're a woman, I can't imagine your wanting a man who doesn't want you. To me, that's insanity. Trying to force someone to love or marry you is irrational and will boomerang on you. It's crazy!

Use your imagination to go about your Father's business, which is letting your wisdom, skill, and knowledge come forth and bless others as well as yourself. You are going about your Father's business if you're operating a small store and in your imagination you feel you're operating in a larger store, giving a greater measure of service to your fellow creatures. If you're a writer of short stories, you can go about your Father's business, creating a story that teaches about the golden rule and the law of love. Using your imaginative faculties, you can create an inspired life that serves yourself and others. You can succeed in all of your endeavors. You can surmount adversity, poverty, and failure.

In a Nutshell

If you wish to be successful, you must first *imagine* yourself as successful. If you wish to be wealthy, you must first *imagine* yourself as wealthy. When the world says, "It is impossible, it can't be done," the person with imagination says, "It *is* done."

Through your faculty to imagine the end result, you have control over any circumstance or condition. If you wish to bring about the realization of any wish, desire, idea, or plan, form a mental picture of fulfillment in your mind.

Constantly imagine the reality of your desire, and in this way you will actually compel it into being. You can imagine abundance where there is lack, peace where there is discord, and health where there is sickness.

Whatever you can conceive, you can achieve. The success that you deeply desire is first an idea in your mind before it takes shape and substance on the screen of space. Using the law of mind and imagination, you can surmount adversity, poverty, and failure and succeed in all of your endeavors.

❄✛❄ ❄✛❄ ❄✛❄

Chapter Six

There's No Free Lunch

*A*s the old saying goes, "There's no such thing as a free lunch." Recently I was in a store that was offering a free pack of razor blades if you bought two tubes of shaving cream. Well, of course, the blades weren't really free—their cost was passed on to the customers indirectly in the price of other things they bought at the store.

Nothing is free. If you want to be wealthy, you must pay the price for wealth; if you want success, there's a price for that. The price of achieving these things is applying the law of mind—and not everyone is willing to do that. For example, I knew a wonderful metaphysical teacher in New York City named Mrs. Menier. She lived in the Lucerne Hotel and had a friend who would visit her, borrow books, and accept the old clothes that were offered to her. I asked Mrs. Menier one time, "Why doesn't this woman listen to you—to your teaching? She doesn't have to wear your old clothes. She could become successful on her own." Mrs. Menier replied, "She's unwilling to pay the price. She's unwilling to pay attention and apply these truths. She prefers old clothes to wisdom."

I think Mrs. Menier was right. Her friend preferred old clothes, secondhand umbrellas, and things of that nature to the application of mental and spiritual laws. All she had to do was take an interest in the great truths, but she was unwilling to pay the price. That's true of many people. Mrs. Menier was very sympathetic and kept on giving her old clothes, but I don't think that actually did her friend any good.

Whatever you desire, you must give your attention, devotion, and loyalty to it. There's always a price to be paid. When you learned to drive, you had to make a conscious effort to learn how to steer, merge, and park. You can probably do all these things effortlessly now. At this point your subconscious mind is actually driving the car. You paid the price by paying attention to learning how to drive a car, and now you can do it automatically.

The price of getting what you want includes having faith that your desires can be fulfilled—and not everyone has this faith. For example, at a summer seminar I was teaching in Denver on the powers of the subconscious mind a few years ago, I met a woman who had been praying for ten years for her eczema to be healed— with no results. She had applied various astringent lotions and other topical medications without any appreciable relief. Although she had tried to be healed, she had never paid the price, which was to have complete faith in the Infinite Healing Presence and the law of her own subconscious—to trust the law and believe that the Healing Presence would respond and heal her skin. She had been giving power to externals, saying, "My skin is sensitive to the sun. I'm allergic to the cold weather. I believe this eczema is spreading all over my arm due to heredity. It's my genes and chromosomes that are at fault." After I explained the importance of having complete faith in the One Power, she began to pray as follows:

> *The Infinite Healing Presence that created my body and all its organs knows all the processes and functions of my body. I claim, feel, and know definitely and absolutely that the grandeur and glory of the Infinite are made manifest in my mind and body. The wholeness, vitality, and life of the Infinite flow through me now, and every atom of my being is transformed by the Infinite Healing Presence. I fully and freely forgive everyone, and I pour out love, truth, and beauty to all my relatives and in-laws. I give thanks for the healing that is taking place now, and I know that when I call, the answer comes.*

She repeated this prayer slowly, quietly, and reverently several times every day. She told me prior to my leaving Denver that a remarkable change for the better had come over her entire being and that her skin had completely healed. She had faith and received the gift of healing.

Faith is attention, devotion, and loyalty to the One Creative Power. You have faith when you know that thoughts are things; that what you feel, you attract; and that what you imagine, you become. You have faith when you know that any idea deposited in the subconscious mind comes forth as form, experience, and conditions. For example, a group of hikers was lost in a forest but had faith that they would be guided to safety. They had no compass and didn't know anything about navigating by the stars, but they sat down and said: "The Lord is my shepherd. I shall not want. He will lead me to safety. He is guiding me now." They followed the lead (an intuition or hunch) that they received from the Supreme Intelligence, and they found their way to safety.

They paid the price by having faith in the Divine Source and calling upon it. Faith comes through understanding the laws of your mind and applying them diligently in all your affairs. Scientists have faith that their research will lead to a greater understanding of nature. Farmers have faith that the seeds they deposit in the ground will result in a harvest. Before you can receive wealth, you must have faith that you will get it. You must impress your subconscious mind with the idea of wealth, for whatever is impressed on the subconscious is expressed on the screen of space.

God is the giver and the gift, and you're the receiver. God is that Infinite Presence and Power, the Life Principle, and the Father of all. God promises: "Call upon me, I will answer you; I'll be with you in trouble and set you on high because you have known my name." The nature of God is to respond to you.

The very fact that you want something is proof that it's already yours. Your act of desiring brings about a response from the Supreme Intelligence within you. The Eternal knows what you need before you even ask. The need is already satisfied; the gift has been given.

You must open your heart and receive. You must get rid of the false beliefs in your mind and accept the truth, which is that the healing power of God is within you. You'll always get a response. Perhaps you've experienced this. You've tried to solve a particular problem. You've wracked your brain, asked others to help you, done the research, and you're exhausted. You finally give up and turn it over to the deeper mind. Then, when you're not thinking about the problem, the answer pops into your mind like bread from a toaster—perhaps while you're dreaming at night or when you're taking a shower.

You pay the price by recognizing that only the Supreme Intelligence knows the answer. When you surrender, turn your problem over to the Source, and say, "There is that within me that knows," the answer comes. Have faith and the Infinite Presence and Power will respond to you.

Thomas Edison had faith that he could develop a lightbulb. He had an intense desire to light up the world and serve humankind, and electricity yielded its secrets to him. He paid the price by persevering and having confidence that the answers would come. He was completely dedicated to his project, knowing in his heart and soul that Divine Intelligence would respond. He kept on keeping on, and his deeper mind never failed him.

Here's another example of how faith in an idea made millions for one man and also helped many others increase their wealth. Sir John Templeton has great faith in his ability to make sound and profitable investments. He was born in 1912 in Tennessee, and in his youth thought he would become a missionary. However, in college he realized that he had a special talent: He was better than most people at investing money. Templeton notes: "It seemed to me that people were making investments based on emotion and ignorance, not common sense."

In the 1940s he developed a group of mutual funds, which was a relatively new concept in those days. In 1954 he founded Templeton Growth Fund, Ltd., which became an extremely successful investment fund. By the time he retired and sold his company in 1992, Templeton had helped thousands of people make money. A $10,000 investment in Templeton Growth made 40 years ago is worth several million dollars today.

Templeton attributes the success of his business to the power of prayer. In an article for the *Positive Living Newsletter,* he wrote: "For 30 years, all directors' meetings of Templeton Growth have opened with prayer, and the investment results for shareholders have not been equaled by any other public mutual funds for those 30 years."

Templeton disagrees with those who argue that he would have been successful even if he had neglected to pray. "My prayer life," he says, "has given me a clarity of mind and a depth of insight that have been the decisive factors in my success. . . . My business colleagues and I don't pray that a particular stock we buy will go up in price, because that just wouldn't work. We simply pray that the decisions we make will be wise ones."

Templeton also established the annual Templeton Prize for Progress Toward Research or Discoveries about Spiritual Realities in 1972 to honor living individuals who have made a major contribution to the expansion of human understanding of divinity. The winner gets more than $1 million—the exact amount is adjusted every year to ensure that it's higher than the amount awarded to Nobel Prize winners. Templeton has stated that he wants his prize amount to be greater to make the point that religion is as important as the arts and sciences. Past winners of the Templeton Prize include Mother Teresa and Billy Graham.

In addition to praying and having faith, it's necessary to focus on love if you wish to achieve your dreams. Love means that what you wish for yourself, you must also wish for others. When you love others, you radiate peace and goodwill to them and rejoice in their success and happiness. In contrast, condemnation and criticism are extremely destructive, generating psychic poison throughout your system, robbing you of vitality, strength, and equilibrium.

I suggested to a musician that in order to become outstanding in his field he should focus on love and pray as follows:

God is the great musician. I am an instrument and a channel for the Divine. The God Presence flows through me as harmony, beauty, joy, and peace. The Infinite Presence and Power plays the eternal melody of love through me. I play the melody of the One Who Forever Is. I am inspired from On High, and majestic cadences come forth, revealing the eternal harmony of God.

Within a few years he became extraordinarily successful. The price he paid was attention, reverence, and devotion to the Eternal Being from whom all blessings flow.

A person who cannot make ends meet must pay the same price of attention and loyalty to the idea of wealth. The price isn't hard labor or burning the midnight oil; it's building the idea of wealth into your consciousness. You can work 14 or 15 hours a day, but if you aren't aware of the Wisdom and Presence within, your labor will be in vain. The kingdom of intelligence, wisdom, and wealth is within you, and when you tap into it, you will have no problem paying your bills. God's infinite ideas are available to you if you tune in and rejoice that Infinite Spirit reveals everything you need to know.

A member of my congregation, Richard D., used the power of the Infinite Almighty to overcome major financial losses. He prayed for guidance and asked that Creative Intelligence reveal what steps he should take to move ahead in his life. He then had an overpowering urge to go into the desert. While musing there, an idea came to him. Richard visualized people leaving Los Angeles and coming out from the East Coast to live in what was then an undeveloped area. In his mind's eye, he saw homes, hospitals, and schools being built there. He shared this idea with an old acquaintance who ran a successful real estate firm in Los Angeles, describing the tremendous potential he saw in that desert. His friend liked his idea and hired him as a salesman to promote the development of that desert land. Richard's success with that project led to a partnership in the firm, and today he has become a multimillionaire in real estate.

Richard paid the price of recognizing the Divine and following the lead that came to him. *You* can also do this. The mere fact that you desire an answer means that the answer is already present in the mental and spiritual world in which you live, move, and have your being. Realize that God is the giver and the gift, and that you must be a good receiver.

Unfortunately, many people are poor receivers. They say, "The good things aren't for me. They're for Mrs. Jones down the street." In fact, everything has been given to you. God dwells within you, and the whole world is yours. Whether you're a sales representative, manager, chemist, or doctor, you can say: "The Infinite Spirit within me reveals better ways in which I can serve. God's creative ideas unfold within me, revealing new and better ways of accomplishing great things and serving humanity." New ideas *will* come to you, but you must have faith, recognize the One Power, and call on it.

A few years ago I helped a waitress learn to use the law of mind to solve a perplexing problem. I met her while I was staying at the Jasper Park Lodge in Alberta, Canada, where she worked. I suggested to her that at night, just before going to sleep, she turn her dilemma over to her deeper mind. I said: "You must recognize that the Infinite Source knows the answer. When you go to it in faith, it will respond. You must pay the price by recognizing this Creative Intelligence."

She spoke to her Infinite Mind this way: "Reveal the answer to me. I know that only you know the answer." She lulled herself to sleep with this prayer, and the next day she received a telegram from Ontario that solved her problem.

The God Presence guides the planets on their course and causes the sun to shine. It's operating in your body, and it takes care of you when you're sound asleep. You must begin to use it. Call upon it and it will respond to you. If you don't call upon it or believe in it, it's just the same as if it didn't exist, for the God Presence will do nothing for you except *through* you—through your own thought, your own imagery, and your own beliefs and convictions.

Barry P. called on this Infinite Power within to become a renowned surgeon. When he was a young intern, he had a serious problem: He was very nervous, which caused his hands to shake. He resolved to overcome this. To steady his hands, he carried a tumbler full of water up and down the stairs for half an hour every day. As the weeks went by, Barry spilled less water each day. It took him six months before he had a steady hand, but he persevered. He paid the price of dedication and became a great eye surgeon.

Would you have given up after a while? Would you have become bored and said, "Oh, I can't be bothered"? Well, Barry wanted to be a good surgeon, and he had to pay the price. Now he's called to Saudi Arabia, England, Ireland, and other places to perform delicate surgeries. He doesn't have to pray for wealth or money—it just flows to him.

Like this surgeon, if you have a desire, you can dedicate yourself and fulfill it. It's natural to desire to be greater than you are—to want health, love, peace, harmony, abundance, and security. If you don't, you're abnormal. Your ultimate desire is to have a sense of oneness with God, called the yoga of love. The Life Principle knows how to bring your dreams to fruition, but you must open your mind and heart and wholeheartedly receive the gift of the One Who Forever Is.

Cast out of your mind all preconceived notions, false beliefs, and superstitions; and realize that when you call, God will answer. You must order your mind and realize that whatever you're seeking already exists in the Infinite Mind. All you have to do is identify your desire, visualizing it as real as your hand or heart.

Struggling and toiling aren't the answers. Having reverence for the Infinite and tapping into it is. I saw a girl dancing at Jasper Park Lodge who invited God to dance through her. It was easy to see the wisdom and rhythm of the Spirit flowing through her, and she received tremendous applause for her performance. She said she was "dancing for God." She deserved the praise uttered. She told me that her teacher told her to always pray that God was dancing through her and that God's grace, ease, and wisdom would always move in her.

Henry Hamblin, the founder of *Science of Thought Review,* also invited God to work through him. At one point in his life, he was facing hard financial times. Walking home under falling snow, he suddenly became aware that the wealth, love, and goodness of God were like the billions of snowflakes falling down all over London. He says, "I opened my mind and heart at that moment to God's Infinite riches, knowing that His wealth, love, and inspiration were like countless snowflakes falling in my mind and heart."

From that moment forward, wealth flowed to him freely and endlessly and he never had financial problems again. He'd changed his mind, and according to his thoughts of abundance, it was done unto him. Nothing else in his environment had changed—London, the snow, and his office were the same—but he had been transformed and became an instrument for the riches of life.

There's no such thing as something for nothing. You must always pay the price—and the price, of course, is attention. Give your attention and love to music, electricity, your job, or anything else; and it will give its secrets to you. That wisdom will be transmitted as you realize that the Infinite is within you and that the Power of God is working through you.

There was an interesting article in the newspaper about Maude Towle, who still gives all her attention to what she loves at age 103. The article said:

> She peers out from behind her Coke-bottle glasses, walking in small, slow steps towards her pride and joy. For most people her age, pride and joy would mean great-grandchildren, or maybe even great-great-grandchildren. But for this 103-year-old woman, the greatest thing in her life is her car, an electric job. Despite the fact that she is 38 years past the retirement age, she recently passed the test for renewal of her California driver's license for the 11th straight year. Maude Towle is one of the ten oldest drivers in the state—but that's just part of her story.
>
> As spry at 103 as most are at 65, she handles payments for a home mortgage company seven days a week. Isn't that wonderful? "I'll never retire," she says, "because if I ever did, I'd starve. They just don't pay enough with Social Security for even an old

person like me to eat these days. This way I never have to apologize to anyone. I can live the way I want and do the things I want without always being told what to do."

It's interesting, isn't it? Maude Towle loves life and contributing to humanity. She's evidence that keeping a love of life and a sense of humor and adventure keeps us young. We only grow old when we become bitter, resentful, and hateful—full of self-condemnation and ill will. These emotions and thoughts corrode our soul, and we grow old. The Life Principle, on the other hand, never grows old. It was never born, and it will never die.

Another person who gave all his attention to what he loved was James Watt, whose invention of the steam engine changed the world. Watt, who was born in Scotland in 1736, earned his living as a repairman in Glasgow. "I could repair nearly every kind of mechanical device," Watt once said. He ran a small workshop and became fascinated with experimenting with steam. In 1763 he did some repairs on a model Newcomen engine, a crude steam engine that consumed a lot of energy and accomplished very little work. While Watt was fixing the engine, he conceived the idea of an entirely new kind of steam engine that would overcome all the faults of the Newcomen. However, he lacked the knowledge to convert his idea into reality. Then a vision came to him one Sunday afternoon in May 1766 while he was walking in a Glasgow park thinking about the engine. Watt recalled: "In the vision I saw a steam engine in complete detail. Before I had walked much further, the whole thing was arranged in my mind."

The next morning Watt went to work. In less than 12 hours, he had built a new engine that efficiently harnessed the power of steam. He patented the idea in 1781, and his invention was soon put to use in factories, triggering the start of the Industrial Revolution.

There are a number of qualities that contribute to personal success in life. Some of these—such as being born to good parents, in a favorable country or social class, or with natural physical and mental endowments—are completely out of our control.

Fortunately, the qualities that really count are the ones that we can cultivate, and the most important of these is *persistence*. If you examine the biography of any man or woman who has made a lasting contribution to humanity, you will find that the majority exercised uncommon persistence.

Let's take the case of Albert Einstein. In grade school he was such an unimpressive student that when his father asked the headmaster what profession young Albert should pursue, the headmaster replied, "It really doesn't matter, because he will never make a success in anything." As we know now, Einstein became one of the greatest physicists of the 20th century, more by reason of determined persistence than because of any natural gifts of genius.

Many similar cases can be cited. For example, in school Winston Churchill was a very slow student. In his early career he was thought to be rather mediocre, and until the crisis of World War II, he had failed to achieve most of his dreams and goals. However, because he had persisted in his chosen path and worked to improve himself, he was prepared when a rare opportunity for leadership came his way at age 66. At a time when most men are retired, he became the British prime minister in 1940 and rallied not only his own countrymen, but also the entire Western world against the threat of the Nazis. Because of his bulldog tenacity, he came to be regarded as one of the greatest political leaders of the 20th century.

Churchill paid the price, didn't he? He focused his attention and refused to give up, always realizing that there is an Infinite Power that responds to one's desires.

Franklin D. Roosevelt was another statesman who persisted and overcame monumental obstacles. He was severely crippled by polio in 1921 and led the United States during the Great Depression and World War II in a wheelchair. One of his great strengths was communicating to the American public through his famous "fireside" radio chats. Although his speeches sounded informal and off-the-cuff, he actually worked doggedly to make them sound so effortless. In a museum in Hyde Park, New York, is a glass case displaying nine drafts of one of Roosevelt's famous speeches. The first was rough, the second improved, and the third improved still further. In the eighth draft only one word had to be changed before the ninth and final draft was run. Think of the hours—perhaps days—that he spent gathering information from experts and putting his speeches together. Of course, his talks had a tremendous influence on the country.

Nothing in the world can take the place of persistence. Talent won't—nothing is more common than talented people who are unsuccessful. Education alone cannot. The world is full of educated derelicts. Only persistence and determination are omnipotent.

Give all of your allegiance and devotion to the God Presence and realize that it's your guide, your counselor, and the source of all blessings. There's no other power. Think of the wonders that would happen in your life if you gave your complete attention and loyalty to that great truth. But if you give power to sticks and stones, to men and women, to the weather, and to all these other things, you're worshiping many different gods and won't get what you want. When you awaken to the truth that there's One Power, One Presence, and One Cause, then your good will flow to you. Now be honest and ask yourself these questions: "Do I really believe in my heart that there is only One Presence, the Living Spirit within me? Do I believe that it's omnipotent and omnipresent? Or do I give power to the external world? Do I give power to the stars, the sun, the moon, the weather, other people, karma, past lives, voodoo, or devils?"

There isn't room for any devil. There's only the One Presence and the One Power. It will be wonderful when you come to that conclusion. When Judge Thomas Troward was asked, "What would you do if all the black magicians were praying against you, pouring out curses?" He responded, "I'd say, 'Cocka-doodle-do.'"

Why did he say this? He knew the "magicians" have no power. The only power is the One Presence moving as unity. There are no divisions or quarrels in it. How could one part of Spirit fight another part of Spirit anywhere in the world? That's the greatest of all truths, my friends. The minute you give power to any other created thing, your mind becomes divided and you're unstable in all your ways.

I read an article about a doctor who was healed from a crippling disease by turning to faith in God. The article reported:

> Dr. Phil Miles once was skeptical about supernatural healing, but no more, for when a bizarre disease attacked his body, gnarling and paralyzing his limbs, it was faith—not modern medicine—that cured him. "It was a miracle," declared the El Paso, Texas, physician. Joy shining in his eyes, he said, "It has given me new life. I'm walking, living, laughing proof that there is a healing force much more powerful than any person on this earth."
>
> For seven years Dr. Miles had suffered from this strange disease, which caused his arms and legs to jerk spasmodically and twist into rigid positions. Dr. Miles, formerly on the staff of the prestigious Walter Reed Army Medical Center, called in some of the finest neurologists in America, but they couldn't even diagnose his illness. Finally, bedridden and growing worse every hour, the heartsick young doctor turned in desperation to his only remaining hope—faith in God. He asked a neighbor to come to his bedside and help him pray for his recovery. The doctor will never forget that incredible day, for every moment of it is etched into his memory.
>
> "I was sobbing uncontrollably as I uttered the words of that prayer," he recalled. "No sooner had the final words left my lips when, to my utter astonishment, my hands, which had been clenched like claws for two days, suddenly began to open. A second later the rigid muscles in my feet began to relax. I realized I was witnessing the power of the Supernatural." He said that within two days he was back on his feet and today, more than two years later, he is still healthy and working again as a specialist in obstetrics and gynecology at William Beaumont Army Medical Center in El Paso, Texas.

Dr. Miles, thirty-six years of age, said the unknown disease struck him without warning. "I was examined by some of the best neurologists in the country, but they couldn't diagnose my illness. In my heart I knew I had a form of multiple sclerosis."

Dr. Miles is a man who paid the price. He tried everything, then surrendered to the God Presence that created him and that knows all things. He called in a neighbor and they prayed together. It was a complete surrender, recognizing the great truth in his heart. He sobbed while he prayed, and there's nothing wrong with that. It shows humility.

Realize that everyone has to pay the price, and that price is attention, recognition, acceptance, and conviction. You can pay the price, too. All you have to do is call upon the Almighty Source, and it will answer you. Let us dwell upon these great truths:

> *My God shall supply all my needs according to His riches and glory. In quietness and in confidence shall be my strength. God richly gives me all things to enjoy. With God all things are possible. Before I call, God answers. According to my faith, it is done unto me. The Lord is my life and my salvation; whom shall I fear? The Lord is the strength of my life; of whom shall I be afraid? God is guiding me now.*

In a Nutshell

Nothing is free. If you want to be wealthy, you must pay the price for wealth; if you want success, there's a price for that. Whatever you desire, you must give your attention, devotion, and loyalty to it; and then you'll get a response, of course. The price is recognition, belief, and conviction. There's always a price to be paid.

Give your attention, devotion, and loyalty to any subject and it will yield its secrets to you. If you don't give your attention to a particular subject—whether it's chemistry, mathematics, or your job—you'll remain in darkness about it.

In order for you to receive, you must first give an idea to your subconscious mind. Before you can receive wealth, you must first impress your subconscious mind with the idea of wealth. Whatever is impressed on the subconscious is expressed on the screen of space.

Cast from your mind all preconceived notions, false beliefs, and superstitions; and realize that before you call, God will answer. Whatever you're seeking already exists in the Infinite Mind. All you have to do is to identify mentally and emotionally with your desire or idea, realizing that it's as real as your hand or heart.

Wisdom is the Presence and Power of God functioning in you. Acknowledge God in all your ways, and He will make plain your paths. Trust and believe in God, and your desires will come to fruition.

☨ ☨ ☨

Chapter Seven

"Why Did This Happen to Me?"

Counseling men and women is a great privilege. It's also an enlightening experience, for it reveals the universal, ordinary difficulties that befall everyone, including broken hearts, job loss, confusion, and loneliness. Sooner or later during the course of a counseling session, the concept of the law of mind enters into consideration, because the knowledge of the awesome truth that "according to your belief, it is done unto you" is the key to a fulfilling life.

Some people, however, believe that their problems are too complicated to resolve with such a "simple" truth. Even veterans of the so-called New Thought movement are often disappointed when I remind them of the law of mind. Invariably, their response is, "Oh yes, that's true. I've known that for years. It's wonderful! But my problem is far too complicated to resolve with such a simple truth." Perhaps they've heard about the law so often that they're wearied by it, and its power no longer resonates in their being. Nonetheless, it's the key to the kingdom of God and always leads to solutions—regardless of the difficulty of the problem at hand.

When someone asks, "Why did this happen to me?" or "Why is my life so complicated by misfortune and unending bad luck?" they're crying out for answers to their confusion and making the oldest, most universal plea for lasting peace of mind. We all have a deep, ingrained desire for the healing balm of truth. Ultimately, we have a longing to experience atonement or "at-one-ment" with God—to live in conscious awareness of our innate, true nature as sons and daughters of a loving, living God.

Although it may appear that we're plagued with numerous difficulties and distresses (and I'm not minimizing them in any way), there's actually only one fundamental disorder: a sense of separation from the universal source of everything, which we have named *God*. Once we understand that there's no separation from God, our other problems become manageable and our fear begins to fade as darkness before the dawn.

Using the law of mind, you mold your own future. It's a vital, transforming process. To anyone who claims that it's "too simple," I have to suggest that *simple* doesn't mean *easy*. Practicing the law of mind requires considerable attention, determination, patience, and responsibility. The amount of time needed to produce results depends on the intensity of a person's interest in the process.

Often, after an initial burst of enthusiasm, people lose interest in applying the law of mind, and their patience fades. They don't want to hear about responsibility and prefer not to be reminded of the simple truth of the One Power and Presence, but it's the key that opens the gates to the kingdom within you. You can make the transforming process hard, unpleasant work—or you can enjoy it as the most exciting time of your life.

There's a legend about a farmer who went to a wise man in his village in Asia and told him about how hard his life was. The farmer didn't know how he was going to survive and wanted to give up. He was tired of fighting and struggling. It seemed like as soon as he had solved one problem, a new one cropped up to take its place.

The wise man asked the farmer to go down to the lake and bring back a bucket of water. He then poured the water into three pots and placed each on a hook over the fireplace. Soon the pots came to a boil. In the first he placed a bunch of carrots, in the second he placed a few eggs, and in the last he placed a handful of tea leaves.

After they boiled for half an hour, he removed the pots from the fireplace. He took the carrots out and put them in a bowl; then he took the eggs out and put them in another bowl. Finally, he poured the tea into a third bowl. Turning to the farmer, he said, "Tell me what you see."

"Carrots, eggs, and tea," the farmer replied.

Then the wise man said, "Pick up the carrots and tell me what you feel."

The farmer did so and said, "The carrots are soft."

Then the wise man told the farmer to take an egg from the bowl and break it. After pulling off the shell, he observed that the egg had become hard. At last the wise man asked the farmer to sip the tea. The farmer smiled as he tasted the fragrant brew.

The farmer then asked, "What does this mean?" The wise man explained that each of these objects had faced the same adversity: boiling water. However, each reacted differently. The carrot went in strong and hard, but after being subjected to the boiling water, it softened and weakened. The egg had been fragile. Its thin outer shell had protected its soft interior, but the boiling water hardened the egg's insides. The tea leaves were unique—as they floated in the boiling water, they had transformed it.

"Which are you?" the wise man asked the farmer. "When adversity knocks on your door, how do you respond? Are you a carrot, an egg, or a tea leaf?"

⊰✞⊱

As you look at the problems you face in your life, ask yourself: "Which am *I*? Am I the carrot that seems strong, but becomes soft and loses strength when faced with pain and adversity? Am I the egg that starts with a fragile heart and a fluid spirit, but becomes hardened and stiff after the loss of a job, a breakup, a financial hardship or some other trial? Or am I like the tea leaf that actually changes the boiling water—the very circumstance that brings the pain?"

When the water gets hot, the tea releases its fragrance and flavor. If you're like the tea leaf, when things are at their worst, you get better and change the situation around you. When the hour is darkest and you're facing a great trial, do you elevate yourself to a higher level?

It's God's plan that all people have enough happiness to make them sweet, enough adversity to make them strong, enough sorrow to keep them human, and enough hope to make them happy. The most joyful people don't necessarily have the best of everything; they just make the most of everything that comes their way. The brightest future will always be based on a forgotten past; you can't go forward in life until you let go of your past failures and heartaches.

When you were born, you were crying and everyone around you was smiling. Live your life so that at the end, you're the one who's smiling and everyone around you is crying. You might want to send this message to those who mean something to you—to people who have touched your life in one way or another; made you smile when you really needed it; made you see the brighter side of things when you were really down; whose friendship you appreciate; and who are so meaningful in your life.

The ancient and venerable masters of wisdom said, "The angels in heaven rejoice when any soul cries out for answers with all their heart and all their soul and all their mind." They said this because sooner or later, every intelligent man, woman, and child has to ask how they are to make sense of this confusing, turbulent world. Asking *why* things happen is the healthiest, most wholesome question possible, I believe.

Many people begin asking this question in the tender years of childhood. Others ask later on—usually when they're feeling disenchanted, weary, or defeated; or when all their noble ideals and ambitions for a better world have begun to fade. *When* we ask isn't as important, however, as *that* we ask. Surely angels rejoice because they know that another person is beginning the most important and fascinating journey of a lifetime, and seeking understanding has become their deepest desire and longing.

Who are these "angels rejoicing in heaven"? The word *angel* derives from the Greek word *angelos*, which means "messenger." Angels are messengers of God's truth or goodness. When an individual is sufficiently evolved—prepared with a ready mind and a willing heart to listen to old, familiar truths presented in new and unfamiliar ways—the angels rejoice.

As the adage says: "When the pupil is ready, the teacher appears." The messenger or teacher arrives in many forms: as a book, lecture, or physician—or even as an apparently "stray" comment. The angel comes in the spirit of truth and speaks to the heart of the supplicant.

No matter what form the angel assumes, welcome the messenger and listen to the message. You have longed to hear the truth—have searched and sought for many years—so don't reject either the form of the messenger or the message itself, even if it's radically, dramatically different from everything that you may have heard and sincerely believed before. *Ye shall know the truth and the truth shall set you free.*

The Bible says that when God finished creating the world, he pronounced it good. You're part of God's creation—an important part. God doesn't play favorites or choose one over another. God can only love everyone equally, and God is within you, willing to do good. The whole or holy tendency of God is to give, heal, and prosper you in every way you're capable of conceiving.

Nothing in the universe can oppose or thwart this will of God. There's only One Presence and Power in which you live, move, and have your being. If you're feeling fearful, believe and know that God is in charge now. God is eternal, infinite truth, and God is leading the way.

In the Sermon on the Mount, Jesus expresses this universal truth: "Ask, and it shall be given you; seek, and ye shall find; knock, and it shall be opened unto you." You will receive truth; angels of every kind will deliver the good news.

It's a sign of spiritual maturity when we acknowledge that our circumstances and problems are of our own creation. The problems that come to you won't necessarily come to me; neither will my particular difficulties ever arrive at your doorstop—and this is as it should be.

There's an old legend that illustrates this concept. A mystic instructed all the people on earth to form a great circle. In the center of the circle they were to deposit all their problems, grievances, misunderstandings, heartbreaks, ailments, lacks, and limitations. They were then told that they could examine this great collection of difficulties and would be allowed to exchange the problems they brought for others.

A great hush fell over the multitudes. They became very still and quiet. After much thought and deliberation, every man and every woman went back to the center of the circle and retrieved their problems, and all returned to the privacy of their own homes. Not one person elected to trade in their own difficulties for the burdens and tribulations of another.

It's so tempting to attempt to solve other people's problems. However, this is a complete waste of our energies. Ultimately we are only equipped to cope with our own lives—for they're of our creation. We can alter and improve them by changing our beliefs and remembering who we truly are: children of God. We must continually remind ourselves to accept our legacy or inheritance of all that's good, true, and beautiful. Then we can enter into perfect peace and the oneness of God.

In a Nutshell

It may appear that we're plagued with numerous difficulties and distresses, but there's actually only one fundamental disorder: a sense of separation from the universal, original source of all—the "Father" that we have named *God*. Once we understand that there's no separation from God, our other problems become manageable and our fear begins to fade as darkness before the dawn.

When a person is sufficiently evolved—prepared with a ready mind and a willing heart to hear old, familiar truths presented in new and unfamiliar ways—a messenger appears and speaks to their heart. As the adage says: "When the pupil is ready, the teacher appears." The messenger arrives in many forms: as a teacher, book, lecture, or physician—or even as an apparently "stray" comment.

You're an important part of God's creation. God doesn't play favorites or choose one person over another. God can *only* love everyone equally, and God is within you, willing to do good. Understanding the law of mind is the key to a fulfilling life, because through your beliefs, you create your future.

This is the essence of many religions: "Ask, and it shall be given you; seek, and ye shall find; knock, and it shall be opened unto you."

᛭✚᛭ ᛭✚᛭ ᛭✚᛭

$Chapter\ Eight$

Praise: A Way to Prosperity

*P*raise is our recognition of the healing presence and power of God within each of us. Praise glorifies God, the Life Principle and Source of the good we desire. Praise always implies radiance and the light of truth—the glorious rays of shining illumination.

Jesus said, "Ye shall know the truth, and the truth shall make you free." When we desire with all our mind, heart, and soul to understand ourselves, a prophet of the truth appears. Then we realize that we become what we contemplate and that, to a great extent, our thoughts control our destiny. With this understanding, we're released from the bondage of false belief, superstition, and dogma. We're no longer captives of the past and are free to enjoy abundant prosperity.

This is the moment we "wake up" to who we really are and understand the incredibly powerful creative aspect of our own contemplations. Until we have this wondrous awakening, we will continue to experience great swings of fortune—from feast to famine, exaltation to despair, and abundance to poverty and lack. When we realize that we're captives in a spiritual and psychological prison of our *own* making, we will be able to break the chains that bind us, throw open the doors, and experience freedom and liberty.

We're here on Earth to recognize our inherent, Divine nature, which is wondrously and powerfully creative. We're here to understand that as we think in our heart (or in modern terms, our *subconscious mind*), so we become. We're perfectly free to program ourselves to expect failure. We can instruct our mind to think that God cannot "save" us or solve our problems. Or we can choose thoughts of success, prosperity, and peace of mind. We can pick our thoughts as coolly and deliberately as we select the clothing we wear each day. We have the God-given right to "wear" the beautiful garment of confidence and expect that our desires will be realized.

We must recognize our innate ability to effect a transformation and know in the depths of our being that we don't have to see ourselves as victims of circumstance—as helpless creatures burdened by unfair demands, unreasonable people, and impossible tasks. We can choose to remain victims or become the victors. We're always capable of reaching higher, more constructive levels of spiritual understanding and awareness.

In the Bible, beauty signifies a balanced state of mind and spiritual maturity. Beauty is a quiet acknowledgment that in some measure, we're now reaping what we have sown in the fertile, creative garden of our mind and heart. Attaining beauty requires courage: It asks nothing less than that we be totally honest with ourselves—that we examine our innermost thoughts and feelings, face them, and (if necessary) heal them.

As we undertake this transformative process, we'll detect repeated patterns—some constructive and some destructive. Sometimes we may not perceive any possible connection between past thoughts and present events, but there always is one. As Kahlil Gibran, the author of *The Prophet*, pondered, "If this is my day of harvest, in what fields have I sowed the seed, and in what unremembered seasons?"

We may have sown some seeds of bitterness and resentment that are now preventing us from experiencing the fruition of our desires for love, prosperity, and peace of mind. In this case, we must learn to forgive. To forgive another is to give ourselves a new perception and vision of life—a new, beautiful garment to wear.

Of course, many people resist forgiving others for past hurts. Rarely does a day go by that a counselor—in whatever field and capacity—doesn't hear, "But you don't know how poorly I've been treated, how much I've been hurt, and the bitterness I've experienced. How can you tell me to forgive?" However, holding on to grudges and resentments only makes *you* unhappy and drains your energy. As I noted in my book *Secrets of the I-Ching*, resentment and a desire to see someone punished corrode the soul and fasten your troubles to you like rivets.

We can deliberately choose to release all resentment against everyone we feel has wronged us and declare a day of freedom for ourselves. We may not approve of or agree with the acts of another, but we must recognize the presence of God in him or her. The same Lord or law of mind is operative in every man, woman, and child who walks the face of the earth. Wisdom is understanding that others are acting from their own personal frame of reference and that sometimes their "wrongdoings" are a reaction to their own hurts and wounds.

We shouldn't think that we're being magnanimous or generous in forgiving others, for we ourselves reap the greatest benefits and rewards in doing so. The most important person to forgive is ourselves. We need to forgive ourselves for having harbored any negative, destructive feelings and resolve not to entertain them in our mind anymore. To do so is to condemn ourselves to prison again, because we literally block our aspirations and prosperity when we hold on to self-condemnation.

Forgiveness lightens and quickens the mind, heart, and soul of humankind. It lifts one of the heaviest burdens we'll ever put upon ourselves, and allows beauty and freedom to shine in our lives. Offering forgiveness and understanding makes us one with God, giving us the fullest possible measure of peace, wisdom, power, and love.

To praise is to practice the presence of God—to exalt and praise the good we desire, in whatever form it may take. To praise is to establish the thoughts of prosperity, love, and peace in our subconscious mind that will manifest as conditions and events on the screen of space.

Praise is offering devotion and attention to our goal. When we praise God, we act in the belief that our good is being unveiled. Praise of God is belief in action.

As we practice the law of mind and live in the highest degree of truth, we will enjoy prosperity and fulfillment. As the Bible says: "Be strong and courageous. Do not be afraid or terrified . . . for the Lord your God goes with you; he will never leave you nor forsake you."

In a Nutshell

Praise is our recognition of the healing presence and power of God within each one of us. Praise glorifies the One Source of the good we desire.

When we desire with all our mind, heart, and soul to understand ourselves, a prophet of the truth appears. Then we realize that we become what we contemplate and that our thoughts and feelings control our destiny. At this moment we're released from the captivity of the past and are free to enjoy prosperity.

We can choose our thoughts and attitude as deliberately as we select the clothing we wear each day. We can focus on thoughts of confidence and positive expectancy—or thoughts of lack and limitation.

We must recognize that we don't have to see ourselves as victims of circumstance—as helpless creatures beset with impossible problems, unreasonable people, and unfair demands. We can choose to remain victims or become the victors.

To praise is to practice the presence of God—to exalt the good we desire, in whatever form we seek. Praise is giving devotion and attention to our goal. Praise of God is belief in action.

※✝※　※✝※　※✝※

Chapter Nine

Why Your Beliefs
Make You Rich or Poor

"*Unto* every one that hath shall be given, and he shall have abundance: but from him that hath not shall be taken away even that which he hath."

Is the above quotation from the Bible cruel or harsh? Are some people destined or chosen to enjoy the riches of this world while others are fated to suffer hardship and deprivation? Absolutely not. This biblical passage is a clear statement about the Creative Power and Presence within us that responds in every moment to our thoughts and meditations, producing the conditions and circumstances of our daily lives. If we focus on prosperity and good, that is what we will generate in our lives. On the other hand, if we focus on lack and limitation, we create scarcity and poverty in our experience.

Those who enjoy the true abundance (constant supply) and prosperity of life are aware of the creative powers of Mind. They understand that as they continually impress their minds with ideas of spiritual, mental, and material abundance, their subconscious mind automatically causes good fortune to be produced in their experience.

This is the great and universal law of life—operative and effective in everyone. This has always been true—and always will be.

Our deep-seated, heartfelt beliefs are manifested as experiences, events, and conditions. If we're convinced that we live in a generous, intelligent, infinitely productive universe governed by a loving God, our conviction will be reflected in our circumstances and activities. Similarly, if our dominant thought is that we're not worthy of Infinite Universal wealth and that we're doomed to remain without, this belief is fulfilled. In short, our overarching mind-set determines whether we're rich in material abundance or poor.

To paraphrase the biblical text, this is why "the rich get richer and the poor get poorer." Once we understand this law, we gain control of our lives, activities, and circumstances. Once we accept the truth that the One Mind is our creative agent, we're well on our way to healing, abundance, prosperity, and health; and we'll find our true purpose and expression in this life.

I know that focusing on prosperity and wealth when one is facing a condition of lack requires some doing—but I also know that it *can* be done. In my book *Your Infinite Power to Be Rich*, I noted that it requires sustained and concentrated effort, but it's worth it because those who practice this disciplined thinking inevitably become rich and can have whatever they want. People who give attention to the limitless riches of Mind—the source of all experiences—will possess more of the good of this world.

Disciplined thinking is the key to using the law of mind. Unfortunately, *discipline* is a word that repels some people. To them, it implies harsh punishment and pain. However, they misunderstand the word's true meaning. Discipline comes from the Latin *disciplina*, meaning *teaching* or *learning*. Discipline of the mind begins when we're eager and yearning for truth. It requires that we examine and understand our heartfelt beliefs and opinions. We need to understand what we believe and why we believe it, and then we can begin to renew our mind and think in a new way.

It can be a shock to recognize that much of the confusion about the abundant life—at least in the Western world—has come to us from scriptures. Many people have been told since childhood, "The Lord loveth the poor." In the Bible, we read: "Blessed are the poor in Spirit: for theirs is the kingdom of heaven," and "It is easier for a camel to go through the eye of a needle, than for a rich man to enter into the kingdom of God."

These words have been spoken from pulpits thousands of times without any consideration or explanation of their true meaning and significance. The words are not meant to be taken literally because the Bible isn't a book of facts. Look upon the Bible as a textbook of metaphysics, however, and you will be on the right track. Scriptural language is rich—replete with practical truths and guidelines that can enrich our experience.

To be "poor in spirit" doesn't mean to be depressed, dejected, and full of despair and sadness. On the contrary, it means that your mind is open and receptive to the truths of God; you have a hunger and thirst to know more and to appropriate more of the Divinity within. It means that you have cleansed your mind of false beliefs, fears, prejudices, and anything and everything that can block your realization of the Divine Presence.

The "rich man," in contrast, is full of intellectual pride, pre-conceived ideas, and dogma about God and Life. He is too pumped up with self-importance to pass through the eye of the needle and enter the realm of God's kingdom, where thoughts are surrendered to the Divine Law.

Poverty is a problem of the mind. Heal the mind, and poverty of all kinds will begin to be eliminated. Government and other institutions will never end poverty until they banish it from the human mind. Of course, we can and should help those who are in need—and there's a way to do it wisely and judiciously. We can help people improve their material conditions and retain their dignity—and we can also help them understand that there are mental and scriptural principles that will enable them to learn, heal, and rid themselves of a sense of poverty. We can help them learn about the One Source, Infinite Intelligence, and Supply within their own minds and hearts.

There's no virtue in poverty; and it's not a crime to be wealthy, if the riches are honestly gained. To rob, defraud, embezzle, or cheat another is to rob from ourselves. Ultimately, it will be done unto us accordingly—sooner or later, in one way or another. The greatest gift and challenge God gives us is the freedom to choose—between good and evil, health and illness, and poverty and abundance. The choice is ours, and we must make it wisely.

There are times when instead of success, we meet failure; instead of abundance, we reap poverty; instead of harmony, we face chaos. When some men and women experience this kind of "bad luck," they wrongly conclude that evil is an infinite power unto itself. On the surface, this may appear to be true. But is it possible that there are two infinities? Mathematically, that cannot be true. There is only One Power, One Source, One Infinite Almighty.

Don't draw your conclusions based on the *appearance* of things. Don't decide based on the way conditions appear at this moment only, for beyond everything that the five senses can detect is God, a living, dynamic, all-intelligent Presence. The ancients called it the *Divine Mind.*

We are always moving between opposites. We experience what is sometimes called the *ups and downs* of life. Moods can swing from euphoria to despair, pleasure to pain, and joy to sadness; but when we recognize and understand that these extremes are manifestations of one principle—of dynamic and constant creation—we will no longer be fearful of the opposites we see all around us and which each of us experiences to a greater or lesser extent. We're here to reconcile these opposites and create harmony, health, and peace in our world.

In my book *Secrets of the I-Ching*, I noted that probably no system of instruction and practical wisdom has a clearer understanding of the principle of opposites than that which the ancient Chinese developed 5,000 years ago! They recognized, understood, and accepted the principle of opposites, which they considered a cycle of change. Everything comes from the Invisible (which they named the Tao or God), remains for a time, and returns to the Invisible.

The Chinese sages concluded that the cosmos—the world, society, and individuals—is always and forever in a constant state of flux, moving from a given state to its opposite. Summer becomes winter; day changes to night; the moon waxes and wanes; the tides ebb and flow; the old dies so that the new may be born.

They acknowledged that there are forces over which we have no control: planetary movements, the season, and the elements. Floods come, endure for a time, and then pass away. Droughts come, endure for a time, and then pass away. Good weather will soon return. It's the natural cycle of renewal and replenishment on a vast, cosmic scale.

The I Ching reveals that all form, shape, and action comes out of the Invisible Tao. We find the same truth in the Judeo-Christian scriptures. The Bible says: "There is no power but of God: the powers that be are ordained by God." The I Ching and the Bible concur that Tao/God functions on a universal plane, in an impersonal manner, according to natural laws or principles.

We're not able to control the elements, but we do have the ability to control and direct our consciousness. We have been blessed or gifted with innate intelligence and the capacity to choose our thoughts, ideas, and attitudes—and that which we long to be, do, have, and share.

These desires are the angels of God, the messengers of the Divine, saying, "Come up higher." Let your desire captivate and hold your attention. You move in the direction of the idea that dominates your mind. We have indeed been given authority— enormous powers over our own lives—but there's an even higher authority to which we can appeal: God, the author of all good.

Recognize that we, of ourselves, can do nothing, but the all-pervading Intelligence and Life Energy is eager and willing to provide, protect, enlighten, and restore us to harmony. It will reconcile opposites and bring us peace of mind. When we have the greatest of all gifts, everything becomes right in our world and we discover heaven—here and now—on Earth.

In the Bible, Jesus teaches about the dualities of life through the parable of the wheat and the tares (weeds). In this story, a farmer plants good wheat seed in his field, but an enemy sneaks in at night and sows weeds among the crop. The farmer's servants ask, "What should we do about the weeds? Should we gather them up?"

The farmer replies, "No, if we try to pull up the weeds, we'll also destroy the wheat. Let them both grow together until the harvest. Then gather the weeds and bind them into bundles and burn them, but gather the wheat in my barn."

Weeds are negative, destructive thoughts and beliefs that don't benefit us in any way. They represent fear, doubt, ill will, resentment, and anger—the desire to get even or gain control or power over others. The parable tells us not to be alarmed when these weeds appear. They come from the mass mind or the collective consciousness that's always with us. Recognize that fact and burn the weeds in the fire of Divine Love. Choose to save only the wheat—the Eternal Verities of life, health, abundance, and true peace.

Have you recently asked, "Why does God allow poverty? Illness? Wars? Death?" Hardly a day passes without hearing these questions in one form or another. They're legitimate questions that we've all asked at some time in our lives, if we think at all.

The answer is that God has given us free will, and as long as we exercise it wrongfully—or with evil intent—these negative conditions will appear again and again. Until we learn the principle of life and accept responsibility for our choices and decisions—individually and collectively—depravity and corruption will continue, and more wars will be fought.

I believe it's a crime that humankind still seeks to acquire things and land by using force and through the devastating horrors of war. There's enough abundance on Earth to provide for everyone, if only we all knew how to claim goodness and prosperity from the Great Provider, and allocated and distributed our resources wisely and judiciously.

Understand the enormous intellectual and emotional powers that you have within your own being. It's a treasure-house and kingdom over which you have been given absolute dominion and authority. Understand the dual nature of the world in which you live, including the ultimate of opposites: life and apparent death. As Emerson said, "Polarity, or action and reaction, we meet in every part of nature."

Throughout our lives we encounter confusing and perplexing dualities. It's a challenge we must face and conquer. It's in your power to use your wisdom, faith, and commitment to do good and make the right choices. In doing so, you will be rewarded with a life of blessings, harmony, and abundance.

We need to recognize that God is love and that it's the nature of love to give. God never withholds our good. We can choose to become ever more receptive; to deepen our understanding; and to heal our sense of separation from Love, Life, and God—with all our minds, hearts, and souls.

In a Nutshell

If we focus on prosperity and good, that is what we will generate in our lives. On the other hand, if we focus on lack and limitation, we create scarcity and poverty in our experience.

Those who enjoy the true abundance (constant supply) and prosperity of life are aware of the creative powers of Mind. As they continually impress their minds with ideas of spiritual, mental, and material abundance—prosperity and plenty—their deeper mind automatically causes abundance to be manifested in their experience.

We live in a universe that's made up of dualities. The greatest gift and challenge God gives us is the freedom to choose—between good and evil, between health and illness, and between poverty and abundance. The choice is ours, and we must make it wisely.

Our moods can swing from euphoria to despair, from pleasure to pain, and from joy to sadness. But when we recognize and understand that these extremes are manifestations of one principle—of dynamic and constant creation—we will no longer be fearful of the opposites that we experience and see all around us.

God has given us free will. As long as we exercise it wrongfully or with ill intent, the world will continue to have corruption, crime, and war. However, when we accept responsibility for our choices and decisions—individually and collectively—evil will disappear.

Chapter Ten

The Golden Rule

"Do unto others as you would have others do unto you." The golden rule is part of all the world's great religions. In fact, it's often called the *essence* of religion. When Hillel, the great Jewish sage who lived in the century before Jesus, was asked what he thought the most important teaching in the scriptures was, he replied, "The most important idea is not to do to your fellow man what you would not want him to do to you." Modern psychologists consider this rule the prime factor in the development of sound interpersonal relations.

What does following the golden rule have to do with becoming wealthy and prosperous? Hillel also answers this question. He said: "If I am not for myself, who will be for me? But if I am only for myself, what am I?" God gives us the power to have wealth and abundance. It's our obligation to make the most of our own talents and opportunities, but we also have the obligation to look out not just for ourselves, but also for others.

When we adopt this attitude as our ethical code and guiding principle, it becomes a dynamic influence in our daily lives. It's the treasure of wisdom within the depths of our being—an inner directive in the heart and soul of every man and woman. We're guided to act in the best ways for all concerned—in our relationships, investments, jobs, and in everything we do. The golden rule is the key that unlocks the blessings in our lives.

The term *golden rule* is not found in any scripture, and the origins of it are obscure. However, its meaning is embodied in Matthew 7:12: "So in everything do to others what you would have them do to you, for this sums up the Law and the Prophets." This is the essence of scriptural offerings: to heal the sense of separation from the One Source that we call God.

It's instructive to learn about how the golden rule is expressed in Eastern teachings as well as in the Judeo-Christian Bible. Approximately five centuries before the birth of Jesus, there was a Chinese philosopher named K'ung-Fu-tzu—better known as Confucius in the Western world. According to his philosophy, a person's primary duty on Earth is to learn from nature and live in harmony with the environment, oneself, and others.

Distressed by the misery and poverty around him, and by dishonesty and waste in government, he concluded that the solution to all these problems was a code of ethics that began with the individual. Confucius reasoned that as an individual improved his conduct, his family, community, and government would also improve and become morally pure and strong.

He was the first of the major religious teachers to enunciate the golden rule, which he stated in the "negative" form: "Do not do unto others what you would not like them to do to you." Note that Hillel stated this in almost the same words several centuries later.

It's obviously wrong to steal, lie, and murder—and according to the golden rule we wouldn't do those things that we wouldn't want done to us. However, it's also important that we actively *do* those things that we would like to have done for us, including offering appreciation, courtesy, and civility. We see examples every day of the lack of these manners in many individuals and families. It's not unusual to hear someone say, "No matter what I do, it's never enough. He (or she) never appreciates it or even says 'Thanks.'"

How often do you say, "Thanks—I appreciate you. I think you're the most wonderful person in the world"? If you want to hear these energizing words, it's wise to say them to others—do it daily until you're comfortable—and really mean them. The golden rule applied is love in action. This may seem simplistic, but try it and you'll be happily surprised. Good relationships or marriages don't "just happen." They must be cultivated, weeded, and nourished if they're to flourish. This is what the golden rule is all about.

You will receive what you give—during difficult times as well as good. We should ask ourselves frequently: "Do I want to receive what I'm giving the other person?" If the answer is yes, that's wonderful. If the answer is no, you should reconsider what you're creating. If you take advantage of another in a business transaction, you had better be prepared for someone to take advantage of you somewhere along the way.

It has been said that those who practice the golden rule are seldom, if ever, caught by surprise. They are forewarned, guided, and protected. They are watched over by the Most High Overshadowing Presence—that all-knowing Intelligence that Confucius called *heaven* or *spirit* and that we call *God*.

When we understand the importance the golden rule has been accorded by most enlightened thinkers, sages, and mystics throughout recorded history, we realize that they were exceedingly wise. They understood the ways of the One Presence—though they called it by various names.

Around approximately the 6th century B.C., there were great spiritual awakenings throughout the Eastern world. Lao-tzu, whose works later became the basis of Taoism, and Confucius were spreading their philosophies in China. The enlightened seers and prophets such as Jeremiah, Ezekiel, and Isaiah were exhorting the Hebrews to keep striving toward their goals as a nation.

During this dynamic period, Mahavira established the tenets of Jainism in India. He was a man of extraordinary awareness. He taught that people must not depend on the clergy or the popular gods of the time, but should instead depend on the One who responds to our meditations.

Mahavira was saddened to see that although people were kind to their friends and associates when all was well and prosperous, as soon as someone suffered a reverse of fortunes or came to grief in some way, their so-called friends frequently disappeared, without offering solace, comfort, and encouragement.

"Don't desert one another," he said. "This isn't right conduct and it isn't wise. For you will be deserted in your time of need. We should regard our companions as our own self—in happiness and suffering, in joy and grief, in good times and bad."

People's difficulties and grief can distress us and even make us feel awkward and uncomfortable, but we should at least make an attempt to comfort them—and not with any expectation of reward—simply because it's the decent and moral thing to do.

Mahavira's expression of the golden rule is perhaps the most compassionate and loving of those that appeared in the six centuries before Christ. Taoism, founded by the gentle Lao-tzu, expresses a similar sentiment: "Regard your neighbor's gain as your own gain; regard your neighbor's loss as your loss." It parallels the biblical injunction: "Thou shalt love thy neighbor as thyself." Applying this rule awakens the faculty or power of compassion—empathy for others, the ability to view them with a larger generosity of spirit and heart, and a greater tolerance for their views and ideas.

We begin to question ourselves: *How would I want my neighbors (and every person with whom I come in contact) to act toward me were our situations reversed? How would I want them to regard my gain: with envy, covetousness, and jealousy? How would I want them to regard my loss? With a total lack of interest? Even with a hidden malice? Even though we may not agree on a given proposition, would I want my neighbors to allow me the right to express an opinion?*

As we contemplate the golden rule, we'll find a certain calmness or gentleness moving within ourselves. We'll also notice that many approach us in a more reasonable and quiet manner. It's a sure sign that compassion, gentleness, and patience are becoming the ruling force within us—a directive from the soul.

Many people I've known have prayed for years for a quiet and peaceful state of mind and for patience—not realizing that one way to achieve these blessings is through practicing compassion. It's a facet of love.

Lao-tzu urged us to commune quietly. Contemplate your union and your neighbor's union with the Tao (God); he will hear you and honor both of you with stillness. *Be still and know that I am God.*

Although some people think of gentleness as weakness, this isn't true. The gentle person is very strong and purposeful. It requires tremendous strength and perseverance to become a gentle being. Extraordinary strength of character is involved. Every one of the avatars and the founders of religions were known for their gentleness. They were powerful enough to change the minds of billions of people and to lead them to strive for better, moral lives.

Although some countries of the East are currently embroiled in conflicts, wars, and acts of terrorism, since the earliest times their religions have taught about the benefits of compassion, tolerance, and personal responsibility for one's behavior toward another. For example, in Sikhism, the golden rule is stated: "As thou deemest thyself, so deem others; then shalt thou become a partner in Heaven."

This statement is attributed to the founder of the Sikhs, Guru Nanak Dev, a former Hindu who sought to dispel superstition and harmonize the most inspired and constructive elements of Hindu and Muslim religious thought in the 15th and 16th centuries. Guru Nanak achieved a wonderful marriage or union of the two religions, emphasizing the belief that there's but One Presence, One Power, One Intelligence; from which all comes and to which all returns. It's known by many names and appellations, but it's ever one and the same, regardless of what we call it.

As thou deemest thyself, so deem others; then thou shalt become a partner in Heaven. This golden rule quietly insists that we adopt a high opinion of others as well as of ourselves, and that we become more lenient and tolerant of their opinions and beliefs, whether or not they conform to our own.

Just as we desire for ourselves the most marvelous freedom of thought and intellectual choice, we must deem it valuable for all others. To become a "partner in Heaven" is to allow others the perfect freedom to think, speak, worship, and vote. It's a partnership in which we are giving at least as much as we expect to receive.

The golden rule is so powerful that if it were universally practiced and applied to all decisions, judgments, and assessments, we would live in a different world. We would create heaven on Earth. If all humankind observed it—collectively and individually—there would be no more war, crime, and cruelty; and no more inhumanity, poverty, and suffering.

By adhering to the golden rule, doing unto others with love and goodwill, we can enrich our lives. We can create a new heaven and a new earth that we may not have known before. We shall receive treasures beyond measure and live in peace, harmony, and plenty in the heaven of our minds and hearts, protected by the Overshadowing Presence or God—the Parent and Lover of all.

In a Nutshell

You will find the golden rule woven like a precious thread through all the major systems of philosophy and religion. It may not appear in the same words, but the intent of the idea is identical: we should treat others as we wish to be treated, and we should allow others the same freedoms of belief, worship, and acquisition that we desire for ourselves.

When we adopt this attitude as our ethical code, it becomes a dynamic influence and energy in our daily lives. It's the treasure of wisdom within the depths of our being—an inner directive in the heart and soul of every man and woman.

The golden rule applied is love in action. Good relationships or marriages don't "just happen." They must be cultivated, weeded, and nourished if they are to flourish. This is what the golden rule is all about.

Various religions emphasize the importance of the golden rule. In Taoism it is said: "Regard your neighbor's gain as your own gain; regard your neighbor's loss as your loss." This statement parallels the biblical injunction: "Thou shalt love thy neighbor as thyself."

Applying this rule awakens the faculty or power of compassion—empathy for others, the ability to view them with a larger generosity of spirit and heart, and a greater tolerance for their views and ideas.

Sikhism also encourages individual tolerance and personal responsibility. *As thou deemest thyself, so deem others; then thou shalt become a partner in Heaven.* This golden rule insists that we adopt a high opinion of others as well as of ourselves, and that we become more lenient and tolerant of their opinions and beliefs, whether or not they conform to our own.

By adhering to the golden rule, we can enrich our lives. We can create a new heaven and a new earth that we may not have known before—a world of compassion, prosperity, and love for all.

Chapter Eleven

Your Future:
The Art of Looking Forward

*L*ooking forward is the art of realizing and demonstrating our inner plans and purposes through our innate, infinite wisdom: the Creative and Healing Presence within. Looking forward is cooperating and living in harmony with the great principles of Life—knowing that all things come forth from the Universal, Infinite Mind or Loving God.

In looking forward, we use our imagination, which is the greatest power there has ever been and ever will be. The Infinite, Creative Presence that we call God always responds to us in accordance with the nature of our inner imaginings and ideas.

We all wonder at times: *What does the future hold for me, my loved ones, and my business or profession? What will become of me?* These questions automatically give birth to more queries: "Are there such things as fate and destiny? Is God responsible for our future? Do we have a say in what will happen to us tomorrow? Are we responsible?"

These are age-old, perennial questions; and every thinking and caring individual asks them. The answers are calling to us now—from within our own hearts—and we're capable of hearing and responding in constructive ways.

In the Bible we read the story of Moses, who after years in exile was tending his flock of sheep at Mount Horeb when he saw a bush burning before him. When the Lord saw that Moses was turning to investigate the bush, he said, "Moses! Moses! Here I am. Do not come any closer. Take off your sandals, for the place where you are standing is holy ground."

As Moses stood before the burning bush, an angel (messenger) of the Lord appeared to him in the flame, commanding him to go to Egypt to free the Israelites from bondage.

The bush that was enveloped in flame is burning within each of us. It's the Divine fire within: our burning desire to rise higher and be more than we are now—to do, give, possess, and express more than in the past. It's the fire that lights the way for everyone who comes into the world.

In the Sermon on the Mount, Jesus said: "You are the light of the world. . . . Let your light so shine before men, that they may see your good works and praise Father in heaven." This is the Divine fire of life—the energy burning within us. It will not consume us or cause us to perish.

Every man, woman, boy, and girl is a flame of the Divine fire—glowing and radiant with possibilities and potential. We're here to become aware of the Divinity within, which is infinitely knowing, intelligent, wise, concerned, and caring.

This discovery and awareness is our primary purpose in life. Once we recognize this, all else falls into place and is harmonized. We can face the future with assurance and equanimity. Truth is inspiring, practical, and pragmatic—and it produces beneficial results.

There are only two ways that we can approach the future: with fear or with faith and confidence in the Infinite Presence that never changes. Our present state of consciousness is "holy ground." This is where we start, with confidence in our wonderful abilities, inborn talents, and noble ideals.

So many of us have been instructed to learn more, read more books, take more classes, and attend more expensive seminars. This can be good and very helpful, but ultimately we have to set what others say to one side and determine our own individual beliefs and opinions. We're called to look within.

Just as Moses spent time in exile in the desert of the Sinai Peninsula, there are times when we have to go into our own interior desert. When we have attempted to do all that we know how to do—when we have utterly exhausted our own resources and feel abandoned and bereft of any sense of hope—then we surrender to the Divine Spirit within.

The desert is a metaphor for our barrenness, when we cannot feel or imagine the waters of spiritual inspiration, intuition, and imagination. This is a recurring, periodic state, and we should not fear it. As the Lord told Moses, we're standing on holy ground. We learn with our mind, heart, and soul that we're not victims of the fears and prejudices that we have inherited from the world.

We need to begin where we are now, and see the biblical desert for what it is: a place of solitary rest, where we can turn away from the confusion, noise, and complexities of a frequently depressing world. Then we can examine the stream and flow of our thoughts. It may surprise us to discover how many of them are about the regretted past and the uncertain future.

Philosophers, psychologists, and religious teachers have advised us for years to live in the present, but very few of us do. We dwell on our past failures and fear the future. However, we're actually always living in the present moment—we can't do otherwise. This is a great truth: When we worry about the future or look back with remorse at the past, we're doing it in the present moment. The past is simply old scenes and events brought into present consciousness. The future has yet to come. Therefore, our thoughts in the present determine whether we're happy or miserable.

Just as Moses was given the directive to deliver the people of Israel to the promised land, we also have a mission. When we understand and accept that we have control of our destiny and fortune, then we will find fulfillment, healing, and a sense of the Living Presence of the Loving God. This is what the future has in store for us: a life more wonderful than we may now know.

God has given us every good thing: the sun, the moon, the stars, and everything necessary to live. It's our responsibility to learn to become good receivers—and to eliminate from our consciousness everything that is contrary and in opposition to our desires, goals, and the "promised land."

Prayer and meditation will help us from being engulfed with resentment, rage, and anger; or filled with the desire for revenge. If these negative feelings arise, become still and rest in the quiet assurance that there's a better way. Forgive yourself and let go! Let the Mind Principle work its perfection. Hear the voice from the burning bush: "I have surely seen the affliction of my people. . . . So I have come down to deliver them from the power of the Egyptians [negativity], and to bring them up from that land, to a land flowing with milk and honey."

When Moses was commanded to lead the Israelites, he asked God to tell him his name so that he would be able to tell the Israelites by whose authority and power he was to lead. God said to Moses, "I am that I am. This is what you are to say to the Israelites: 'I am has sent me to you.'"

I am is a declaration of conscious being—uttered by all men and women. When you say *I am,* you declare the presence of the Living God within you. The word *that* indicates that which you want, desire, and would like to be.

Who do you say you are when you say *I am?* Do you say, "I am fearful, afraid, poor, and unhappy"? Or do you become still and respond, "I am a child of the Living, Loving Presence. I am destined to become greater than ever before. I am Divinely guided to my ideal place in life, where I express myself at my highest capability and become a blessing to all humankind"?

Resolve to eliminate from your conversations sentences such as, "I'm afraid," "I'm poor," or "I'm sick," because they deny the very ideals that we desire to express. Speak with confidence and assurance. Contemplate *I am,* and the spark of faith will become a flame—a burning fire that lights all of our activities and affairs.

God is eternal—ageless and timeless. The timelessness in you is aware of the Divine Almighty's timelessness. The Infinite Presence within knows that yesterday is but today's memory, and tomorrow is today's dream. Remind yourself a thousand times a day: *God is always with me* and *I am a beloved child of the Loving Father.*

With a belief in the One Power and One Source, you will overcome poverty and lack, and have faith that you will be successful. You will purge all thoughts of poverty and need from your mind, and program your subconscious for a future of well-being, prosperity, and accomplishment.

In a Nutshell

Every man, woman, boy, and girl is a flame of the Divine fire—glowing and radiant with possibilities and potential. We're here to become aware of the Divinity within, which is infinitely knowing, intelligent, wise, concerned, and caring.

There are only two ways that we can approach the future: with fear or with faith and confidence in the infinite and universal principles that never change. When we understand and accept that we have control of our destiny and fortune, then we will find fulfillment, healing, and a sense of the Living Presence of the Loving God. Life has a wonderful future in store for us.

Resolve to eliminate phrases such as, "I'm afraid," "I'm poor," or "I'm sick" from your conversations. In making such statements, you deny the very ideal and good that you desire to experience. Instead, speak with confidence and assurance about your wonderful abilities, perfect health, and noble ideals.

Contemplate *I am* or the Infinite Presence, and the spark of faith will become a flame—a burning fire that always lights your way. Yesterday is but today's memory, and tomorrow is today's dream. Let today embrace the past with quiet remembrance, and look to the future with longing love.

⊶✝⊷ ⊶✝⊷ ⊶✝⊷

Biography of Joseph Murphy

Joseph Murphy was born on May 20, 1898, in a small town in the County of Cork, Ireland. His father, Denis Murphy, was a deacon and professor at the National School of Ireland, a Jesuit facility. His mother, Ellen, née Connelly, was a housewife, who later gave birth to another son, John, and a daughter, Catherine.

Joseph was brought up in a strict Catholic household. His father was quite devout and, indeed, was one of the few lay professors who taught Jesuit seminarians. He had a broad knowledge of many subjects and developed in his son the desire to study and learn.

Ireland at that time was suffering from one of its many economic depressions, and many families were starving. Although Denis Murphy was steadily employed, his income was barely enough to sustain the family.

Young Joseph was enrolled in the National School and was a brilliant student. He was encouraged to study for the priesthood and was accepted as a Jesuit seminarian. However, by the time he reached his late teen years, he began to question the Catholic orthodoxy of the Jesuits, and he withdrew from the seminary. Since his goal was to explore new ideas and gain new experiences—a goal he couldn't pursue in Catholic-dominated Ireland—he left his family to go to America.

He arrived at the Ellis Island Immigration Center with only $5 in his pocket. His first project was to find a place to live. He was fortunate to locate a rooming house where he shared a room with a pharmacist who worked in a local drugstore.

Joseph's knowledge of English was minimal, as Gaelic was spoken both in his home and at school, so like most Irish immigrants, Joseph worked as a day laborer, earning enough to keep himself fed and housed.

He and his roommate became good friends, and when a job opened up at the drugstore where his friend worked, he was hired to be an assistant to the pharmacist. He immediately enrolled in a school to study pharmacy. With his keen mind and desire to learn, it didn't take long before Joseph passed the qualification exams and became a full-fledged pharmacist. He now made enough money to rent his own apartment. After a few years, he purchased the drugstore, and for the next few years ran a successful business.

When the United States entered World War II, Joseph enlisted in the Army and was assigned to work as a pharmacist in the medical unit of the 88th Infantry Division. At that time, he renewed his interest in religion and began to read extensively about various spiritual beliefs. After his discharge from the Army, he chose not to return to his career in pharmacy. He traveled extensively, taking courses in several universities both in the United States and abroad.

From his studies, Joseph became enraptured with the various Asian religions and went to India to learn about them in depth. He studied all of the major faiths and their histories. He extended these studies to the great philosophers from ancient times until the present.

Although he studied with some of the most intelligent and farsighted professors, the one person who most influenced Joseph was Dr. Thomas Troward, who was a judge as well as a philosopher, doctor, and professor. Judge Troward became Joseph's mentor and introduced him to the study of philosophy, theology, and law as well as mysticism and the Masonic order. Joseph became an active member of this order, and over the years rose in the Masonic ranks to the 32nd degree in the Scottish Rite.

Upon his return to the United States, Joseph chose to become a minister and bring his broad knowledge to the public. As his concept of Christianity was not traditional and indeed ran counter to most of the Christian denominations, he founded his own church in Los Angeles. He attracted a small number of congregants, but it did not take long for his message of optimism and hope rather than the "sin-and-damnation" sermons of so many ministers to attract many men and women to his church.

Dr. Joseph Murphy was a proponent of the New Thought movement. This movement was developed in the late 19th and early 20th centuries by many philosophers and deep thinkers who studied this phenomenon and preached, wrote, and practiced a new way of looking at life. By combining a metaphysical, spiritual, and pragmatic approach to the way we think and live, they uncovered the secret of attaining what we truly desire.

The proponents of the New Thought movement preached a new idea of life that is based on practical, spiritual principles that we can all use to enrich our lives and create perfected results. We can do these things only as we have found the law and worked out the understanding of the law, which God seems to have written in riddles in the past.

Of course, Dr. Murphy wasn't the only minister to preach this positive message. Several churches, whose ministers and congregants were influenced by the New Thought movement, were founded and developed in the decades following World War II. The Church of Religious Science, Unity Church, and other places of worship preach philosophies similar to this. Dr. Murphy named his organization The Church of Divine Science. He often shared platforms, conducted joint programs with his like-minded colleagues, and trained other men and women to join his ministry.

Over the years, other churches joined with him in developing an organization called the Federation of Divine Science, which serves as an umbrella for all Divine Science churches. Each of the Divine Science church leaders continues to push for more education, and Dr. Murphy was one of the leaders who supported the creation of the Divine Science School in St. Louis, Missouri, to train new ministers and provide ongoing education for both ministers and congregants.

The annual meeting of the Divine Science ministers was a must to attend, and Dr. Murphy was a featured speaker at this event.

He encouraged the participants to study and continue to learn, particularly about the importance of the subconscious mind.

Over the next few years, Murphy's local Church of Divine Science grew so large that his building was too small to hold them. He rented the Wilshire Ebell Theater, a former movie theater. His services were so well attended that even this venue could not always accommodate all who wished to attend. Classes conducted by Dr. Murphy and his staff supplemented his Sunday services that were attended by 1,300 to 1,500 people. Seminars and lectures were held most days and evenings. The church remained at the Wilshire Ebell Theater in Los Angeles until 1976, when it moved to a new location in Laguna Hills, California.

To reach the vast numbers of people who wanted to hear his message, Dr. Murphy also created a weekly radio talk show, which eventually reached an audience of over a million listeners. Many of his followers suggested that he tape his lectures and radio programs. He was at first reluctant to do so, but agreed to experiment. His radio programs were recorded on extra-large 78-rpm discs, a common practice at that time. He had six cassettes made from one of these discs and placed them on the information table in the lobby of the Wilshire Ebell Theater. They sold out in the first hour. This started a new venture. His tapes of his lectures explaining biblical texts, and providing meditations and prayers for his listeners, were not only sold in his church, but in other churches and bookstores and via mail order.

As the church grew, Dr. Murphy added a staff of professional and administrative personnel to assist him in the many programs in which he was involved and in researching and preparing his first books. One of the most effective members of his staff was his administrative secretary, Dr. Jean Wright. Their working relationship developed into a romance, and they were married—a lifelong partnership that enriched both of their lives.

At this time (the 1950s), there were very few major publishers of spiritually inspired material. The Murphys located some small publishers in the Los Angeles area and worked with them to produce a series of small books (often 30 to 50 pages printed in pamphlet form) that were sold, mostly in churches, from $1.50

to \$3.00 per book. When the orders for these books increased to the point where they required second and third printings, major publishers recognized that there was a market for such books and added them to their catalogs.

Dr. Murphy became well known outside of the Los Angeles area as a result of his books, tapes, and radio broadcasts, and was invited to lecture all over the country. He did not limit his lectures to religious matters, but spoke on the historical values of life, the art of wholesome living, and the teachings of great philosophers—from both Eastern and Western cultures.

As Dr. Murphy never learned to drive, he had to arrange for somebody to drive him to the various places where he was invited to lecture in his very busy schedule. One of Jean's functions as his administrative secretary, and later as his wife, was to plan his assignments and arrange for trains or flights, airport pickups, hotel accommodations, and all the other details of the trips.

The Murphys traveled frequently to many countries around the world. One of his favorite working vacations was to hold seminars on cruise ships. These trips lasted a week or more and would take him to many countries around the world. In his lectures, he emphasized the importance of understanding the power of the subconscious mind and the life principles based on belief in the one God, the "I AM."

One of Dr. Murphy's most rewarding activities was speaking to the inmates at many prisons. Many ex-convicts wrote him over the years, telling him how his words had truly turned their lives around and inspired them to live spiritual and meaningful lives.

Dr. Murphy's pamphlet-sized books were so popular that he began to expand them into more detailed and longer works. His wife gave us some insight into his manner and method of writing. She reported that he wrote his manuscripts on a tablet and pressed so hard on his pencil or pen that you could read the imprint on the next page. He seemed to be in a trance while writing. He would remain in his office for four to six hours without disturbance until he stopped and said that was enough for the day. Each day was the same. He never went back into the office again until the next morning to finish what he'd started. He took no food or drink while he was working. He was just alone with his thoughts and his huge library of books, to which he referred from time to time. His wife sheltered him from visitors and calls and took care of church business and other activities.

Dr. Murphy was always looking for simple ways to discuss the issues and to elaborate points. He chose some of his lectures to present on cassettes, records, or CDs, as technologies developed in the audio field.

His entire collection of CDs and cassettes contains tools that can be used for most problems that individuals encounter in life. His basic theme is that the solution to problems lies within you. Outside elements cannot change your thinking. That is, your mind is your own. To live a better life, it's your mind, not outside circumstances, that you must change. You create your own destiny. The power of change is in your mind, and by using the power of your subconscious mind, you can make changes for the better.

Dr. Murphy wrote more than 30 books. His most famous work, *The Power of Your Subconscious Mind,* which was first published in 1963, became an immediate bestseller. It was acclaimed as one of the best self-help guides ever written. Millions of copies have been sold and continue to be sold all over the world.

Among some of his other best-selling books were *Telepsychics— The Magic Power of Perfect Living, The Amazing Laws of Cosmic Mind Power, Secrets of the I-Ching, The Miracle of Mind Dynamics, Your Infinite Power to Be Rich,* and *The Cosmic Power Within You.*

Dr. Murphy died in December 1981, and his wife, Dr. Jean Murphy, continued his ministry after his death. In a lecture she gave in 1986, quoting her late husband, she reiterated his philosophy:

> I want to teach men and women of their Divine Origin, and the powers regnant within them. I want to inform that this power is within and that they are their own saviors and capable of achieving their own salvation. This is the message of the Bible and nine-tenths of our confusion today is due to wrongful, literal interpretation of the life-transforming truths offered in it.
>
> I want to reach the majority, the man on the street, the woman overburdened with duty and suppression of her talents

and abilities. I want to help others at every stage or level of consciousness to learn of the wonders within.

She said of her husband: "He was a practical mystic, possessed by the intellect of a scholar, the mind of a successful executive, the heart of the poet." His message summed up was: "You are the king, the ruler of your world, for you are one with God."

HAY HOUSE TITLES OF RELATED INTEREST

DIVINE MAGIC: The Seven Sacred Secrets of Manifestation,
revised and edited by Doreen Virtue, Ph.D.

EVERYDAY WISDOM FOR SUCCESS, by Dr. Wayne W. Dyer

HOW SUCCESSFUL PEOPLE WIN: Using "Bunkhouse Logic"
to Get What You Want in Life, by Ben Stein

INTENTIONAL WEALTH: The Secrets
of Effortless Prosperity, by Colette Baron-Reid

THE LAW OF ATTRACTION: The Basics
of the Teachings of Abraham, by Esther and Jerry Hicks

THE LITTLE MONEY BIBLE, by Stuart Wilde

QUANTUM SUCCESS: The Astounding Science
of Wealth and Happiness, by Sandra Anne Taylor

꙰✛꙰

All of the above are available at your local bookstore,
or may be ordered by contacting:

Hay House USA: **www.hayhouse.com**®
Hay House Australia: **www.hayhouse.com.au**
Hay House UK: **www.hayhouse.co.uk**
Hay House South Africa: **www.hayhouse.co.za**
Hay House India: **www.hayhouse.co.in**

✠

We hope you enjoyed this Hay House book.
If you'd like to receive a free catalog featuring additional
Hay House books and products, or if you'd like information
about the Hay Foundation, please contact:

Hay House, Inc.
P.O. Box 5100
Carlsbad, CA 92018-5100

(760) 431-7695 or (800) 654-5126
(760) 431-6948 (fax) or (800) 650-5115 (fax)
www.hayhouse.com® • www.hayfoundation.org

✠

Published and distributed in Australia by: Hay House Australia Pty. Ltd.,
18/36 Ralph St., Alexandria NSW 2015 • *Phone:* 612-9669-4299
Fax: 612-9669-4144 • www.hayhouse.com.au

Published and distributed in the United Kingdom by: Hay House UK, Ltd.,
292B Kensal Rd., London W10 5BE • *Phone:* 44-20-8962-1230
Fax: 44-20-8962-1239 • www.hayhouse.co.uk

Published and distributed in the Republic of South Africa by:
Hay House SA (Pty), Ltd., P.O. Box 990, Witkoppen 2068
Phone/Fax: 27-11-467-8904 • orders@psdprom.co.za • www.hayhouse.co.za

Published in India by: Hay House Publishers India,
Muskaan Complex, Plot No. 3, B-2, Vasant Kunj, New Delhi 110 070
Phone: 91-11-4176-1620 • *Fax:* 91-11-4176-1630 • www.hayhouse.co.in

Distributed in Canada by: Raincoast, 9050 Shaughnessy St.,
Vancouver, B.C. V6P 6E5 • *Phone:* (604) 323-7100 • *Fax:* (604) 323-2600
www.raincoast.com

✠

Tune in to **HayHouseRadio.com®** for the best in inspirational talk radio
featuring top Hay House authors! And, sign up via the Hay House USA
Website to receive the Hay House online newsletter and stay informed
about what's going on with your favorite authors. You'll receive bimonthly
announcements about Discounts and Offers, Special Events, Product
Highlights, Free Excerpts, Giveaways, and more!
www.hayhouse.com®